Desktop Publishing

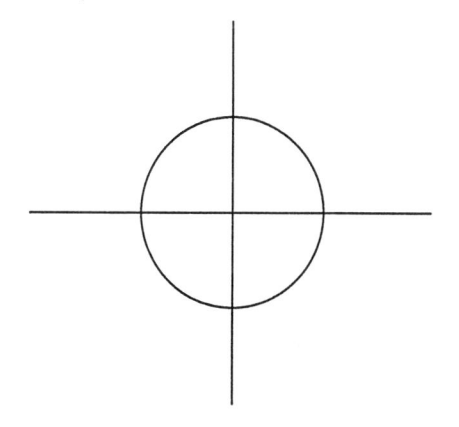

Design Basics

Desktop Publishing

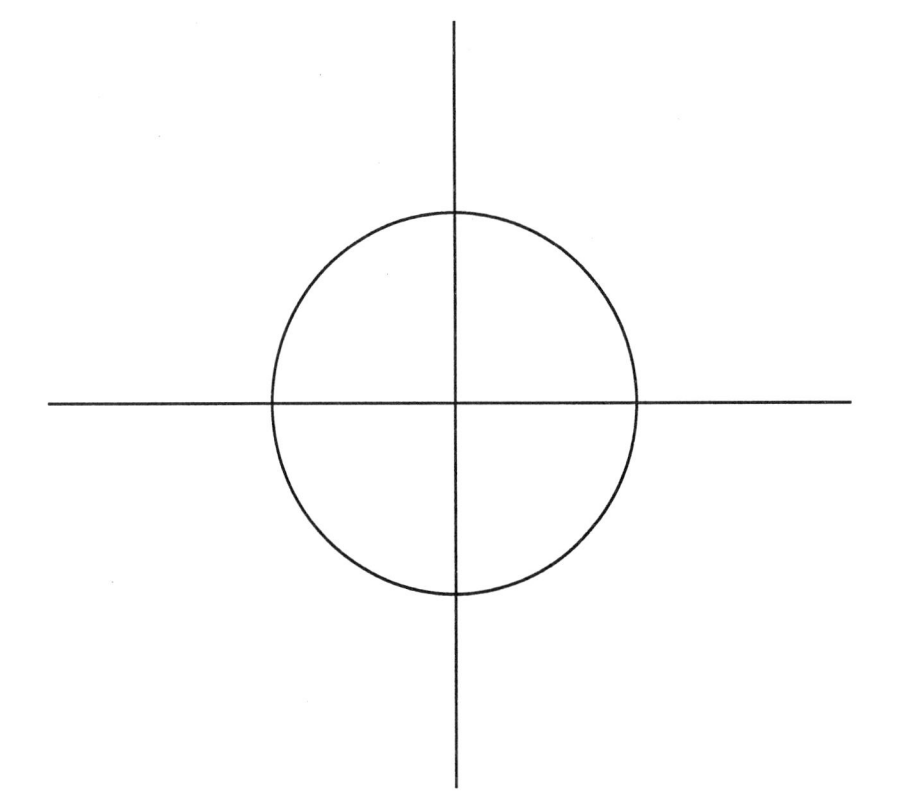

Design Basics

Alan Holmes Charles Lubelski Ivor Powell Keith Ranger

© Watford College, 1989

All rights reserved. No part of this book may be reproduced or utilised in any form or by any means, electronic or mechanical, including photocopying, recording or by an information storage and retrieval system, without permission in writing from the publisher.

Published in the United Kingdom by
 Blueprint Publishing Ltd
 40 Bowling Green Lane
 London EC1R ONE
 Tel. 01-278 0333

British Library Cataloguing in Publication data
Desktop publishing: design basics
 1. Publishing. Applications of computer
 systems
 070.5'028'5

ISBN 0-948905-42-5

Printed in Great Britain by The Ipswich Book Company, Ipswich, Suffolk.

Contents

Introduction	
Basic Design Principles	1
Measurement Systems	5
Style of the House	7
Margins	9
Grids	13
Copyfitting	17
Headings and Sub-headings	19
Typeface Terminology	25
Typefaces	27
Justification Styles	35
Indenting Styles	37
Letterspacing	39
Rules and Boxes	41
Producing a Document	47
Selection of Founts	49
Typeface Specimen Charts	55

Introduction

These materials were originally developed by staff at Watford College as a result of work done under an Education Support Grant programme for information technology in further education and were intended to assist staff in colleges and in companies who require guidance on design considerations, layout and typographical knowledge for personal computers used for desktop publishing production.

The book may be used by trainers in industry or by college staff to assist student work on short courses or as part of full-time courses leading to external or internal awards.

Although some additional material has been added to help widen the scope of the book, there has been no attempt to reach upwards to those who already have a sound design background and the content is still directed solely towards those uninitiated in the disciplines and traditions of design and layout.

Similarly, to keep the price of the book at a reasonable level for such purposes, there has been no attempt to re-generate material to produce a book which is, in itself, an example of faultless design. The content derives from various sources and has been produced on several different DTP systems.

Acknowledgements

Watford College is grateful to the many companies and organisations who have given permission to quote from and use copyright material for these notes.

Basic Design Principles

Symmetrical Design. This is often regarded as the simplest design form and one which beginners may be advised to use first in order to produce a pleasing result. It has certain basic aspects – e.g. all lines are centred in the space available; therefore the shape of all material appearing to the left of the central axis is reflected by that appearing to the right of it.

To create such a design, the designer has to make choices about the relative importance of the elements contained in it and give corresponding emphasis through choice of typeface, size and style.

As mentioned elsewhere, it is wise to restrict the number of different typefaces used in any one job, as many typographic effects can be achieved through using only size differences and bold, medium, italic, capitals or lower case variations of the same typeface. Symmetrical designs are often seen as being rather staid, conservative, unexciting and 'old fashioned', but they are safer to use when one is not skilled enough in typographic design to experiment more widely.

```
                Watford College Publications



        Basic Design Principles

              A Handbook of Ideas


                    1988-89








              Hempstead Road, Watford
```

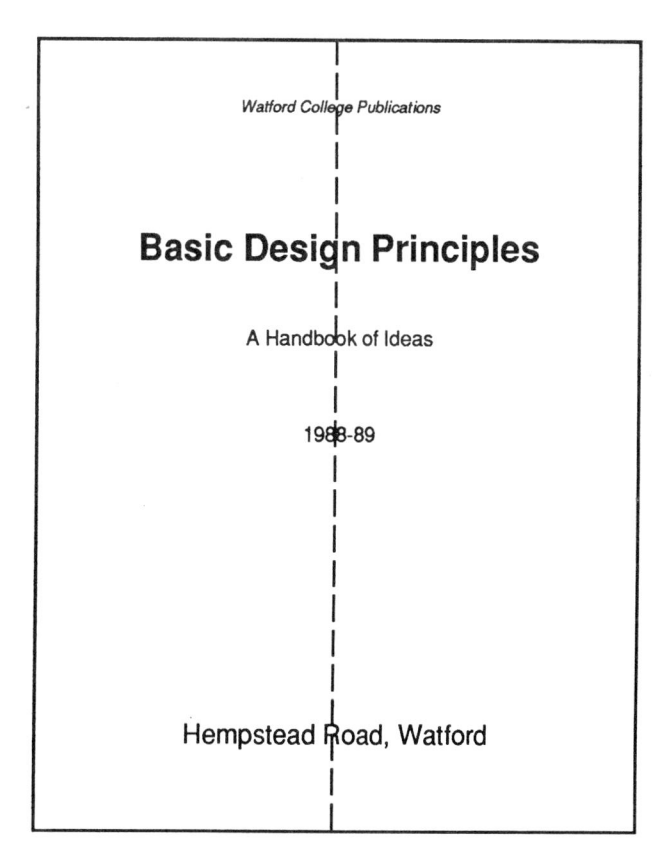

An example of a symmetric design, using one typeface only.

Asymmetrical Design. This is more difficult to achieve than the symmetric one. The reason is that for it to be successful it needs to have a good balance between space and printed area. It still requires a choice of relative importance between the various elements as in symmetric design but it is the placement of those elements with the space which determines its success. It is sometimes known as 'off-centred' design because often there will appear an axis of balance, either to the left or right of centre, apparent by the lining up of various elements. One method of achieving this balance between printed areas and space is to sub-divide the whole area into smaller ones which are in the same proportion and then make the printed areas conform to them.

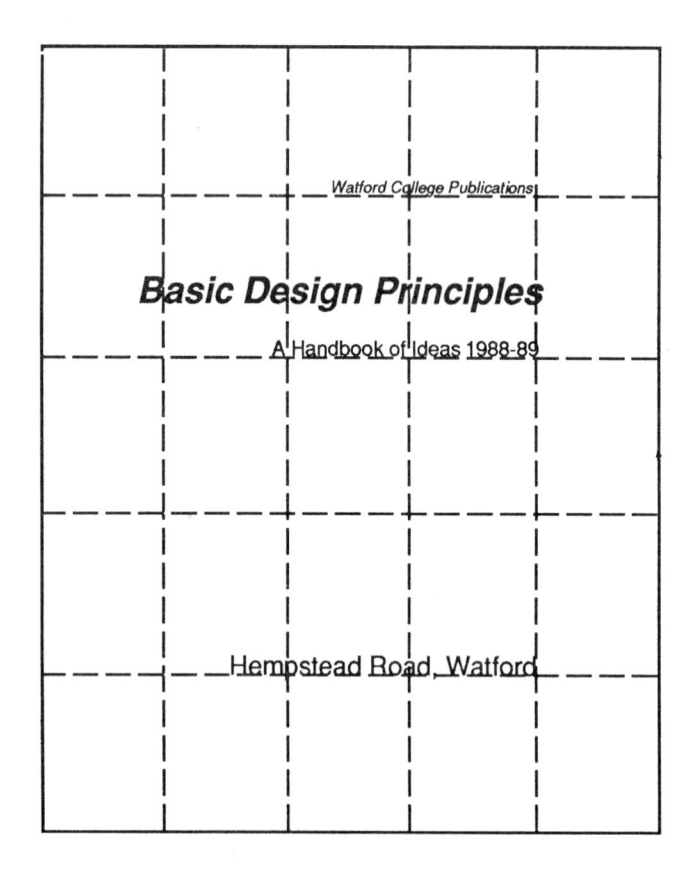

Watford College Publications

Basic Design Principles

A Handbook of Ideas 1988-89

Hempstead Road, Watford

Optical Centre. This is an important concept in design and it relates to a point in a rectangular space which is centrally placed at about two-thirds of the way up the available space. It is this point which attracts the viewer's eye when looking at an upright rectangle — more so than the geometric centre, which is much lower. To achieve maximum effect, the most important part of a simple design should be placed at this position.

Geometric Centre

Optical Centre

Measurement systems

The Point System

Traditionally, typesetters and printers have used a unique measuring system which bore no direct relationship to any other. Most of the English-speaking world uses the Anglo-American Point System in which the basic unit is called a Point.

The Point measures 0.35 mm (originally 0.013837 inch).

As the Point is a small increment it is useful for measuring small items but not so useful for longer dimensions such as the width or depth of a page. There is, therefore, a secondary unit for linear measurement which is called a Pica.

The relationship between the two units is that 1 Pica = 12 Points.

In practice, it is only small items like type sizes, thicknesses of rules or inter-line spacing which are measured in Points. Dimensions of pages, lengths of rules or dimensions of borders are measured in increments of the Pica.

Type size in Points

The type used on this page is 10 pt with 1 pt of extra space between lines.

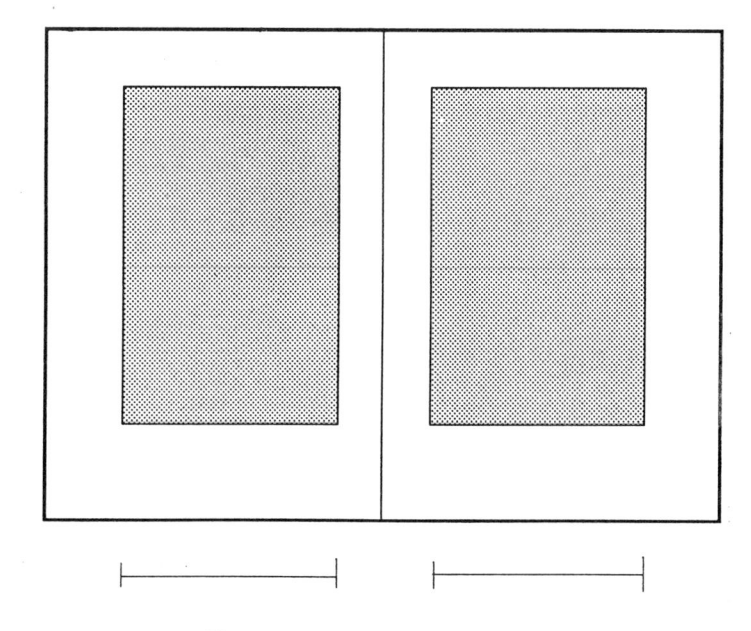

Type page dimensions in Picas

Special rulers, known as typescales, are made for this purpose and, usually, these will be graduated in Picas and Points as well as metric measurements.

The Didot System

Whereas the Point System is used throughout the UK and the USA, on the Continent of Europe they use the Didot System.

This system, which pre-dates the Point System, uses the Didot as its basic unit and at 0.376 mm, it is slightly larger than the Point.

The unit of linear measurement in this system is called the Cicero, which is equal to 12 Didots.

The Metric System

With the increased use of PC-driven composition systems by personnel without a technical typesetting background, the Metric System is now widely used for type measurement.

This is the result of working with photocomposed material where the limitations imposed by the casting of metal type no longer apply.

Imperial Measurements

In the United States, however, where the Metric System has not been so widely adopted, it is common to find systems still using the inch as a type measuring unit.

Style of the house

People concerned with the preparation of text matter for printing must produce it in a consistent style. They should adopt a set of rules which are called the 'Style of the House'.

The main reason for this is to maintain a consistency of style throughout the work. It should be applied to all work except in circumstances where the customer requires a different style from that of the house.

Print buyers have the right to insist upon their own Style of House, or deviate from that of the printer. This can become something of a problem. For example, one publisher may prefer the 'ise' spelling whilst another may insist upon the 'ize' in such words as 'recognise'/'recognize'. One publisher may require all abbreviations to be printed without full stops, whilst another one will complain if a single stop is omitted.

Where a typesetter has to produce text in accordance with a different style than the official one, a printed style sheet or booklet should be produced for each customer. This should prevent the typesetter or proofreader deviating from the style required by the publisher.

Sometimes copy is received from various sources. For example, newspapers receive their copy from professional journalists or ordinary members of the public. Compliance with a Style of the House when the text is typeset should eradicate all inconsistencies of spelling, date styles, punctuation, hyphenation, etc. used by the various authors. These can all be standardised according to the rules of the style. It may cover such things as the use of punctuation, abbreviations and contractions; the spelling of words where there are alternatives; the use of capital letters, bold type, italic, etc; the use of numerals; spacing; and rules to be followed when breaking words.

It may take the form of a small printed booklet or a sheet but in many cases it is simply determined by unwritten custom within a company. It is advisable to have a printed style as this will save confusion and error as well as enabling a number of keyboard operators to be employed on one job without differences arising in the style of type setting.

In the absence of an accepted style in a particular establishment the *Rules for Compositors and Readers at the University Press, Oxford*, or the *Authors' and Printers' Dictionary* are good sources.

Typical extracts from a Style of the House are as follows:

Indention

The first paragraph of text should not be indented, but the second and subsequent paragraphs should be indented by one em (approximately two characters). This rule applies to the first paragraph of text following a sub-heading. In this publication new paragraphs have not been indented but extra space has been inserted between paragraphs.

Abbreviations
Full stops should generally be used with abbreviations and contractions, except where they end with the same letter as they would have done if they were spelt out in full, e.g. 1st Jan. 1995.

Spacing
No extra space should be used after full stops or any other punctuation mark.

Figures and Numerals
Numbers under 100 should be spelt out in text setting, commas should be inserted where necessary when a number contains four or more figures e.g. 3,000.

Use of Italics
Italics should be used for the titles of books, periodicals, newspapers, plays and films, etc. when set in the text. Foreign words used in the English language should be italicised except where they have become accepted as English words.

Division of Words
Words should be broken after a vowel and the second portion should generally start with a consonant e.g.natu-ral. Sufficient of the word should be placed before the hyphen to give the reader some idea of what is coming. When a word has a double consonant the hyphen may be placed between them. Every effort should be made to avoid having a divided word as the last word of a page. Words which have only one syllable should not be divided but where the word is made up of two, three or four syllables the word is normally divisible between the syllables. Word breaks should be avoided at the end of more than two successive lines.

Hyphens
Use sparingly at all times. Omit the hyphen in today, tomorrow and tonight. Hyphens should be used in the spelling out of fractions e.g. one-half, two-thirds and in numerals e.g. twenty-three, ninety-eight. Use hyphens in compound adjectives such as up-to-date model, the boarded-out child.

Margins

Margins set-off and enhance the type area.

The margins on a pair of pages of a book, or a magazine or any printed matter help to focus the eye on the type area. Our eyes are accustomed to certain conventions and any marked deviation from 'conventional' margins means an interruption in the flow of reading.

Margins are subject to the laws of proportion. Specific formulae can be applied so that text areas can be set to both classical and conventional proportions. Classical book margins have their origins in early manuscripts in which the foot margin was about twice the head margin; the foredge was an average of the top and foot together, and the back was half the foredge. While these proportions are no longer strictly followed they do form a good guide and can easily be modified to suit the type of work required.

Prestige and expensive publications generally have large margins. Clearly, large margins mean fewer words per page, thus requiring more pages in the publication and obviously greater paper costs.

When planning margins the following should be considered:

Always consider the layout in pairs of pages, that is as a left hand page (verso) and a right hand page (recto).

Carefully consider the method of binding: saddle stitch and ring bound work require larger back (spine) margins.

Allow for page numbers (folios) and running heads.

The two following examples are typical proportions and measurements for single column pages (note a pair of pages).

A5

Text area 27 picas wide and 41 picas deep. Head margin 3 1/2 picas, foot margin 6 picas, back margin 3 picas, foredge margin 5 1/2 picas.

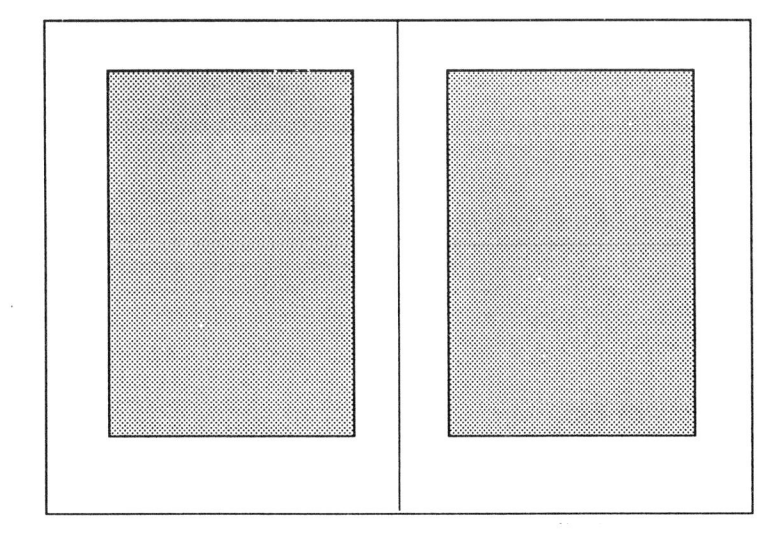

A4
Text area 39 picas wide and 55 picas deep. Head margin 6 picas, foot margin 9 1/2 picas, back margin 4 picas, foredge margin 7 picas.

If ring or comb binding is required then extra room for binding can be achieved by using the last formula but moving the left hand page so that it occupies the same dimensions as the right hand page. Both back margins would be 20 picas, both foredge margins would be 4 3/4 picas.

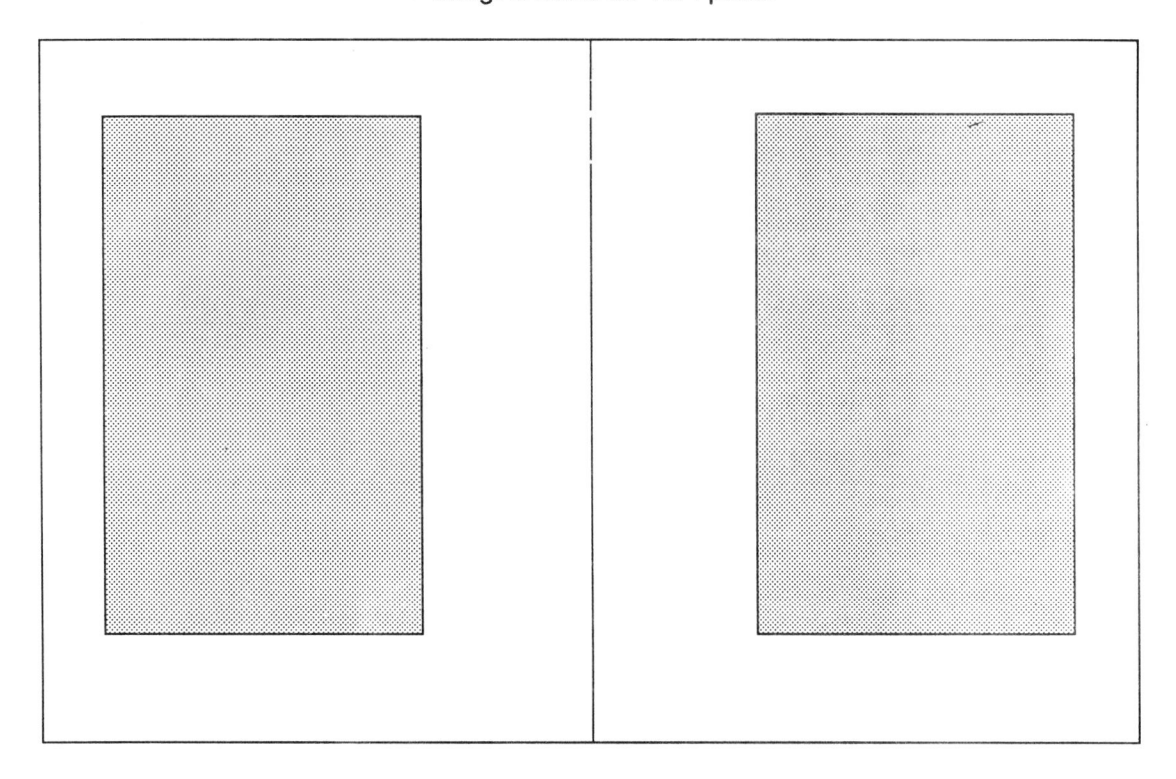

General printed matter

Printed material consists of two components, (a) the text and graphic area (b) the margins or white space area surrounding the printed matter. There several rule-of-thumb guides (as previously indicated). Large margins suggest quality or expensive work, but are uneconomical. Narrow margins are economical but do not set-off the printed matter with the same effect as wide margins. If you can be generous with margins then do so, A wide margin will improve the aesthetic appearance of the printed material. However, when economic factors need to be considered or that the particular job demands narrow margins. then use them. A mass produced leaflet or similar ephemeral matter will be perfectly suited to a narrow margin layout. Expensive looking brochures or items of stationery would clearly look much better with wider margins.

Modern or asymmetric margins can improve the look of a document or booklet. This type of margin is especially useful for A4 pages when small diagrams, illustrations or subsidiary text is required. The specific proportions can vary with each document but a typical pair of A4 pages would be as follows: text area 25 picas wide and 58 picas deep, head margin 5 picas, foot margin 8 picas, left back margin 4 3/4 picas, right back margin 20 picas, left foredge 20 picas, right foredge 4 3/4 picas.

Grids

Grids are a production aid and a design tool. The preparation of a working grid is advisable when dealing with large amounts of complex information. Even for relatively simple work a grid system is a definite advantage.

Bookwork, brochures, magazines, catalogues can all be advantageously designed using a grid system designed to deal with a variety of graphic and typographic elements.

In one sense the grid is no more than a ruler – a way of dividing up space into a commonly understood language, thus enabling the designer, illustrator, typographer and printer to position 'graphic elements' into a fixed or pre-arranged area of a page.

Thus, main textual areas, side headings, headlines, footnotes, illustrations and the like, can be fitted into a reserved area on a page.

The type of grid and the format (page size) are, to a certain extent, dependent on each other and the choice of both grid and format depends very much on the type of printed material to be presented.

For example, a paperback novel and a telephone directory are made up of pages of type. But there the similarity ends. They are designed quite differently because of the nature of the text or information contained in them. It would be very difficult to understand a novel if it was produced in the type size and columns used in the telephone directory.

In a traditionally designed book (you have already studied a simple grid system in the previous chapter on margins) the grid is simple: the page area is a standard width and depth and there is a right and left hand page. However, as the 'elements' of a page increase and become more complex so too must the grid.

A great deal of thought and preparation must go into the construction of a grid as every 'element' must be catered for i.e. headings, text, illustrations, folios (page numbers), margins, bleeds, tables and tabular work. Typesizes for headings, sub-headings, cross heads, main text areas, side or footnotes, captions. Choice of typefaces and leading (interlinear space) are also important considerations.

Grid designs inevitably vary according to the requirements of each individual job. The different permutations and possibilities of using grid designs are enormous but this system of design need not be applied to each and every design problem.

A further refinement with grid systems is to work to a mathematical ratio basis whereby margins, gutters (the space between columns) and balancing white areas all bear some relationship one to the other. The simplest grid is to use 12 point (pica) vertical and horizontal lines, but 6 point, 18 point and centimetres units can also be used.

The following are common A4 grid formats which can be modified to suit particular documents. Note that function and visual appearance are the most important criteria in the final choice of a grid structure.

A typical A4 three column grid
Text area of three columns of 13 picas and 1 pica in gutters (the space between columns). Head margin 5 picas, foot margin 8 1/2 picas, back margin 4 picas, foredge margin 5 picas. The column depth is 57 picas. These dimensions can be modified to suit individual documents and books. The text matter can be justified (that is set to the full column measure – all lines) or set unjustified (range to the left with an unequal right hand margin).

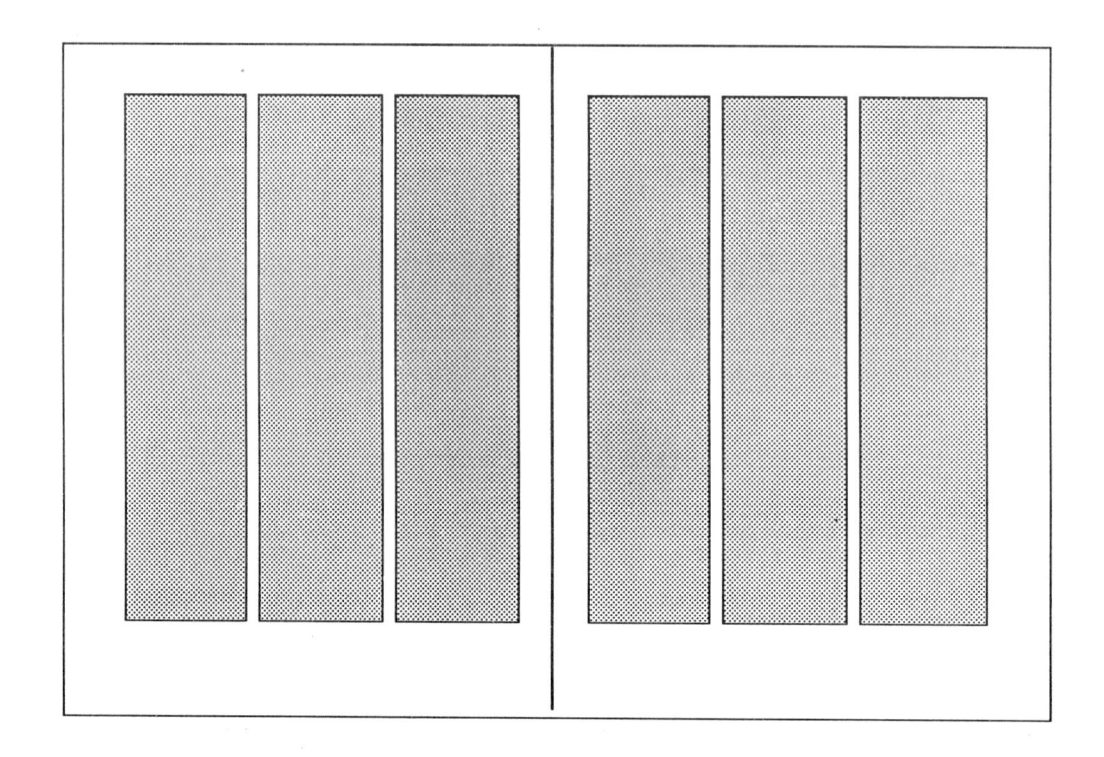

Desktop Publishing: Design Basics

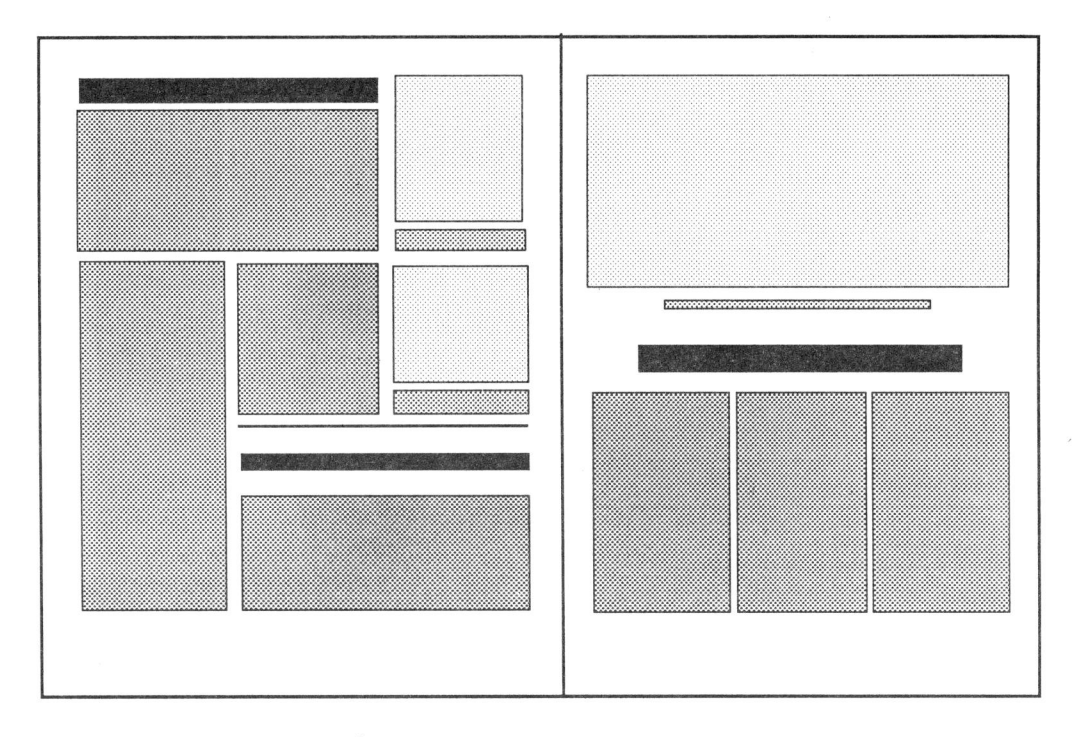

key:

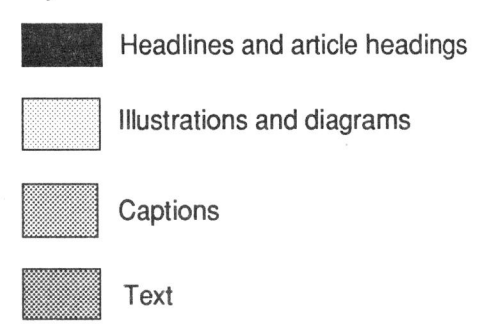

■ Headlines and article headings

☐ Illustrations and diagrams

▨ Captions

▓ Text

The above pair of pages demonstrate how the graphic and typographic elements are controlled by the grid system.

Copyfitting

The amount of printed matter that a quantity of copy will make when typeset often needs to be ascertained before typesetting commences.

The principal reason for 'casting off' copy before production commences is to prepare an accurate estimate of quantities and cost. The amount of type matter will determine other quantities such as how many pages the type is likely to make; how many plates will be needed; and how much paper will be required.

There are several methods that can be employed to cast off an amount of copy. They include the Test Portion, Character Count, and by using Copyfitting Tables.

The Test Portion Method

This is where a small amount of copy is set in the required typeface and size and a proportional calculation is carried out.

For example, if the copy contains 5,000 words and 200 of those words make exactly 7 lines of type, the type will make approximately 175 lines of type (5,000 — 200 = 25 × 7 = 175 lines of type).

Another proportional calculation for this system is based on the number of lines of copy used and type set rather than a certain number of words. The keyboard operator must stop setting where a line of type finishes at the same word as in the line of copy.

For example, if the copy contains 100 lines and a test portion setting shows that 20 lines of copy ends evenly with 25 lines of type, the number of lines of type that the copy will make when set will be about 125 (100 — 20 = 5 × 25 = 125 lines of type). If there are to be 28 lines of type on each page there will be 5 pages of type (125 — 28 = 4 13/28 = 5 pages of type).

Character Count

This method is based on the assumption that the average English word contains five characters, plus one word space between it and the word next to it.

The principle of this method is that the character content of one page of type is divided into the character content of the copy (which in fact is the number of characters and spaces). For example, if the content of one page of type was 2400 characters (comprising an average of 60 characters on one line of type × 40 lines of type) and the copy contained 48,000 characters (8,000 words × 6 [average number of characters per word + one word space]) the number of type pages that the job will make would be 20 pages (48,000 characters — 2,400 characters).

The disadvantage of this system is that it is based on assumptions and averages and consequently is not very accurate.

Copyfitting Tables

These provide the best and most accurate system of casting off. Tables are published and can be purchased (or be created). They give the average number of characters that are contained in one line of type when set in a given type face in a given type size and measure. Although the system is based on averages, the average number of characters contained in one line of type has been scientifically calculated and will prove to be most accurate.

The principle of this method is that after calculating the number of characters in the copy, the total is divided by the average number of characters contained in one line of type (this figure being obtained by referring to the casting off tables). This will provide the number of lines of type that will be set and therefore if divided by the number of type lines that are to appear on each page, will give the number of pages that it will make.

For example, if there are 48,000 characters in the copy and the casting off tables show that on average there are 24 characters in one line of type there will be 2,000 lines of type when set (48,000 — 24 = 2,000). If there are to be 40 lines of type matter on each page there will be 50 pages of type in the publication (2,000 type lines — 40 lines per page = 50 pages of type).

pica ems		5	6	7	8	9	10	11	12	13	14	15	16	17	18	19	20	21	22	23	24	25	26
PLANTIN 110	6pt	18.8	22.6	26.4	30.1	33.9	37.7	41.5	45.2	49.0	52.8	56.6	60.3	64.1	67.9	71.6	75.4	79.2	83.0	86.7	90.5	94.3	98.1
	8pt	15.6	18.7	21.8	25.0	28.1	31.2	34.3	37.5	40.6	43.7	46.8	50.0	53.1	56.2	59.3	63.7	65.7	68.7	71.8	75.0	78.1	81.3
	9pt	14.2	17.1	20.0	22.8	25.7	28.5	31.4	34.2	37.1	40.0	42.8	45.7	48.5	51.4	54.2	57.1	60.0	62.8	65.6	68.5	71.4	74.2
	10pt	13.8	16.6	19.4	22.2	25.0	27.7	30.5	33.3	36.1	39.4	41.6	44.4	47.2	50.0	52.7	55.5	58.3	61.0	63.8	66.6	69.4	72.2
	11pt	12.9	15.5	18.1	20.7	23.3	25.9	28.5	31.1	33.7	36.3	38.9	41.5	44.1	46.7	49.3	51.9	54.5	57.1	59.7	62.3	64.9	67.5
	12pt	11.2	13.4	15.7	17.9	20.2	22.4	24.7	26.9	29.2	31.4	33.7	35.9	38.2	40.4	42.6	44.9	47.1	49.4	51.6	53.9	56.1	58.4

pica ems		5	6	7	8	9	10	11	12	13	14	15	16	17	18	19	20	21	22	23	24	25	26
TIMES	6pt	19.2	23.0	26.9	30.7	34.6	38.4	42.3	46.1	50.0	53.8	57.6	61.5	65.3	69.2	73.0	76.9	80.7	84.6	88.4	92.3	96.1	100.0
	8pt	15.8	19.0	22.2	25.3	28.5	31.7	34.9	38.0	41.2	44.4	47.6	50.7	53.6	57.1	60.3	63.4	66.6	69.8	73.0	76.2	79.3	82.5
	9pt	14.4	17.3	20.2	23.1	26.0	29.0	31.8	34.7	37.6	40.5	43.4	46.3	49.2	52.1	55.0	58.0	60.8	63.7	66.6	69.5	72.4	75.3
	10pt	13.3	16.0	18.6	21.3	24.0	26.6	29.3	32.0	34.6	37.3	40.0	42.6	45.3	48.0	50.6	53.3	56.0	58.6	61.3	64.0	66.6	69.3
	11pt	12.5	15.0	17.5	20.0	22.5	25.0	27.5	30.0	32.5	35.0	37.5	40.0	42.5	45.0	47.5	50.0	52.5	55.0	57.5	60.0	62.5	65.0
	12pt	10.8	13.0	15.2	17.3	19.5	21.7	23.9	26.0	28.3	30.4	32.6	34.7	36.9	39.1	41.3	43.4	45.6	47.8	50.0	52.1	54.3	56.5

pica ems		5	6	7	8	9	10	11	12	13	14	15	16	17	18	19	20	21	22	23	24	25	26
UNIVERS LIGHT 685	6pt D	18.5	22.2	25.9	29.6	33.3	37.0	40.7	44.5	48.2	51.9	55.6	59.3	63.0	66.7	70.4	74.1	77.8	81.5	85.2	89.0	92.6	96.2
	8pt D	14.9	17.9	20.9	23.9	26.9	29.9	32.8	35.8	38.8	41.8	44.8	47.8	50.8	53.7	56.7	59.7	62.7	65.7	68.7	71.6	74.6	77.6
	9pt D	12.7	15.2	17.7	20.3	22.8	25.3	27.9	30.4	32.9	35.5	38.0	40.5	43.0	45.6	48.1	50.6	53.2	55.7	58.2	60.8	63.3	65.8
	10pt D	11.0	13.2	15.4	17.6	19.8	22.0	24.2	26.4	28.6	30.8	33.0	35.2	37.4	39.6	41.8	44.0	46.2	48.4	50.6	52.8	55.0	57.2
	12pt D	9.5	11.4	13.3	15.2	17.2	19.1	21.0	22.9	24.8	26.7	28.6	30.5	32.4	34.3	36.2	38.1	40.0	41.9	43.8	45.7	47.6	49.5

It may be seen from the above casting off table that if the copy is to be set in 10 pt Times to a column width of 18 picas (3 inches or approximately 76 mm), there will be an average of 48 characters per line. It therefore follows that if there are to be 40 lines of type on each page there will be about 1,920 characters (48 characters × 40 lines) on each page. From this figure it is simple to calculate how many pages the publication will contain and thereby how much paper will be required to produce it.

Headings and sub-headings

In text matter where the chapters are long and the subject somewhat complex, it is quite normal for subheadings (subheads) to be inserted into the text as a guide to the reader. Page numbers (folios) can be placed at the top or bottom of the page either in the centre or to the outside of the page but never positioned near to the back margin of the book.

Subheadings in conventional bookwork tend to follow a formal style with limited variations whereas in displayed material there can be more imaginative usage. In either circumstance consistency is important.

Our examples on the following two pages demonstrate conventional usage; we then give some guidelines for more adventurous possibilities.

Subheading Style 1

In text matter where the chapters are long and the subject somewhat complex, it is quite normal for subheadings (subheads) to be inserted into the text as a guide to the reader. Page numbers (folios) can be placed at the top or bottom of the page either in the centre or to the outside of the page but never positioned near to the back margin of the book.

Subheading Style 2 In text matter where the chapters are long and the subject somewhat complex, it is quite normal for subheadings (subheads) to be inserted into the text as a guide to the reader. Page numbers (folios) can be placed at the top or bottom of the page either in the centre or to the outside of the page but never positioned near to the back margin of the book.

Subheading Style 3

In text matter where the chapters are long and the subject somewhat complex, it is quite normal for subheadings (subheads) to be inserted into the text as a guide to the reader. Page numbers (folios) can be placed at the top or bottom of the page either in the centre or to the outside of the page but never positioned near to the back margin of the book.

Caption Style 1
Normally set in 8 point Roman or Italic.

Caption Style 2
Normally set in 8 point Roman or Italic.

Desktop Publishing: Design Basics

Shoulder notes are normally set in a type size that is 2 points smaller than the text and positioned level with the first line of the text.

Why is it necessary to design a printed publication and why should it be created by a competent designer? One might just as well ask, 'Why is it necessary to prepare a plan for a proposed building and why should this plan be prepared by an architect?' Any inexperienced D.I.Y. person can put up some sort of shack. Any desk top publisher can create the pages of a document. But who wants to live in a shack?

It would be far better for the publisher to consider and plan the elements of the pages before creating the document. The tools of the operator's trade are the type of paper and its colour, size and shape; colour of the printed image; the face/s and size/s

Cut-in notes are positioned on the right hand side of the page and set in a small type size that is ranged to the left.

of type to be used; the number and widths of columns that will construct the page grid*; the margins of white space between the columns of type and the paper edges; the style and form of illustrations; binding materials and methods; and so on.

Once the publication has been designed and planned satisfactorily it can be sent for production with confidence with the likelihood that the whole publication will appear interesting and readable. After all, this is what is required from a piece of printing. Think how nice it would be not to live in a shack!

Why is it necessary to design a printed publication and why should it be created by a competent designer? One might just as well ask, 'Why is it necessary to prepare a plan for a proposed building and why should this plan be prepared by an architect?' Any inexperienced D.I.Y. person can put up some sort of shack. Any desk top publisher can create the pages of a document. But who wants to live in a shack?

Marginal notes should align with the text to which it refers. Set in a type size that is smaller than the text.

It would be far better for the publisher to consider and plan the elements of the pages before creating the document. The tools of the operator's trade are the type of paper and its colour, size and shape; colour of the printed image; the face/s and size/s of type to be used[1]; the number and widths of columns that will construct the page grid; the margins of white space between the columns of type and the paper edges; the style and form of illustrations; binding materials and methods; and so on.

Once the publication has been designed and planned satisfactorily it can be sent for production with confidence with the likelihood that the whole publication will appear interesting and readable. After all, this is what is required from a piece of printing. Think how nice it would be not to live in a shack!

The number and length of footnotes should be limited. The footnote should be in reference to the text that appears above it on the page. Standard reference marks (e.g. [1][2][3] or *) should be used as identifying marks. Type pages, including the footnotes, must be the same depth as the standard page. The footnotes should be set in a size at least 2 points smaller than the text.

* For information on this subject see elsewhere in this document.
[1] For information on this subject see elsewhere in this document.

The headings and sub headings in a document are there to focus the reader's attention on a given subject. The headings should therefore be easy to read and attract attention.

1. Use a type style that gives emphasis, e.g. a bold typeface.

> **Visibility**

2. Do not underline — it looks amateurish.

> **Visibility**

3. Use a type style slightly larger than the text. This also helps to give emphasis.

> **Visibility**
>
> ***A sub-heading***
> This is the text below the subheading. The change in size helps to give emphasis to the main heading and the sub-heading.

4. Put extra space above and below headings, but not in equal proportions. Always have more space above a heading than below. This helps to group the heading with its relevant text.

> This is an example of a subheading placed into a block of text matter. It is essential that the visual space above each sub-heading is considerably more than the space below the sub-heading.
>
> ***Visibility***
> The visual effect of the line spacing is to group the subheading with its relevant text. One line of space above and below the heading would not give this effect.

5. Do not use too many capital letters in headings. It is often more readable if the headings are all in upper and lower case letters.

> **Visibility**
>
> **VISIBILITY**

Note: Insignificant words in headings such as 'in', 'at', 'on', 'by' etc., should not have capital letters.

> **Visibility of the text** ✓
>
> **Visibility Of The Text** ✗

6. Do not put full stops at the end of headings. This is unnecessary and often creates an imbalance.

> **Visibility of the text.** ✗

7. Do not indent the first paragraph under a heading. The paragraph indent is to show the start of a new subject. The heading provides this, and an indent looks untidy and lacks balance.

> *Visibility*
> Do not indent the first paragraph under a heading. The paragraph indent is to show the start of a new subject. The heading provides this and an indent looks untidy and lacks balance. ✓

> *Visibility*
>   Do not indent the first paragraph under a heading. The paragraph indent is to show the start of a new subject. The heading provides this and an indent looks untidy and lacks balance. ✗

8. Keep a standard style of justification for headings throughout a document e.g. all ranged left or all centred.

Visibility

      Visibility

           Visibility

9. When reversing out (white on black), or when placing words on top of a tinted area, some loss of definition occurs. To help to reduce this:
   a. Use a bold type face
   b. Do not use type faces that have very thin strokes to the letters.
   c. Use a fairly large type size.

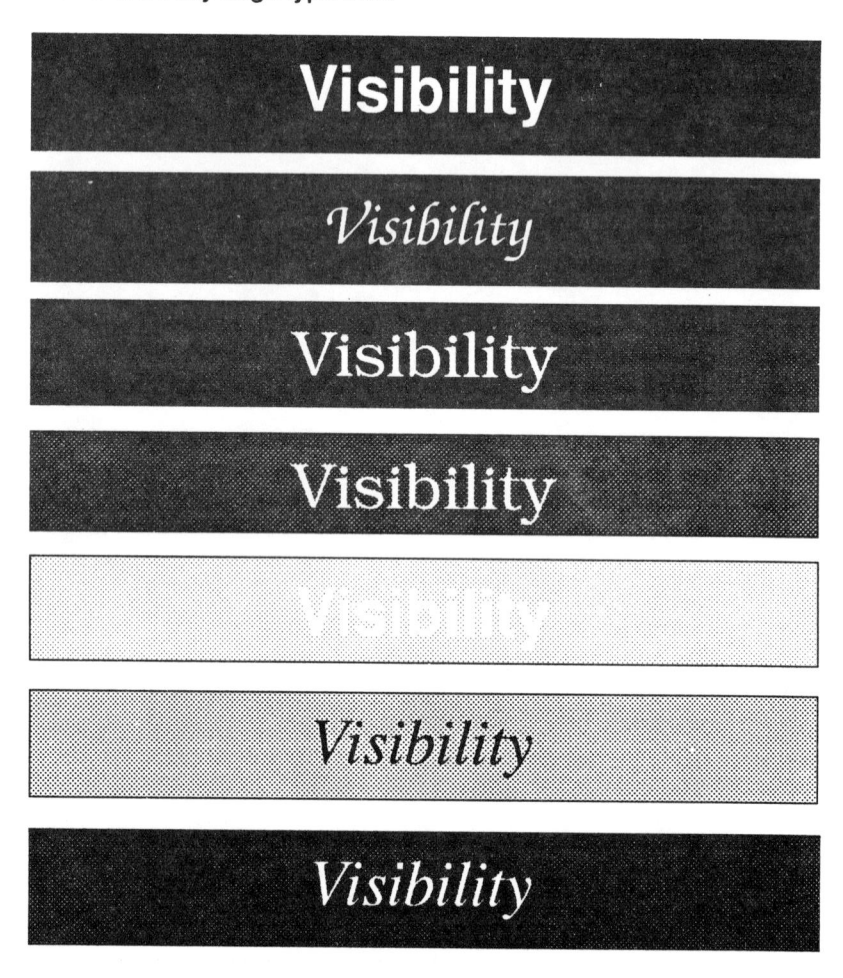

Typeface terminology

The word *type* is derived from the Greek word *typos*, which loosely translated means *letterform*. Today the word is used both individually and collectively to refer to the letters of the alphabet as well as anything else used to create words, sentences, or typographic display.

Individual letters, figures, and punctuation marks are called *characters*. The capital letters are called *uppercase* characters or *caps* and are indicated by 'u.c.' or simply 'c.'. The small letters are called *lowercase* characters and are indicated 'l.c.'. When uppercase and lowercase characters are combined, such as the text being used here, they are indicated 'u/l.c.' (upper and lowercase) or 'c/l.c.' (caps and lowercase).

Other terms with which the designer should be familiar are:

Baseline
The line on which all the capitals and most of the lowercase characters appear to stand.

X-Height
The height of the body, or main element, of the letterform. The x-height is actually the height of the lowercase letter x.

Ascender
The part of the lowercase letter that rises above the x-height.

Descender
The part of the lowercase letter that falls below the baseline.

Counter
The enclosed or hollow part of the letter.

Serif
The short stroke that projects from the ends of the main strokes. Not all type has serifs; type without a serif is called *Sans Serif*, which is French for 'without serif'.

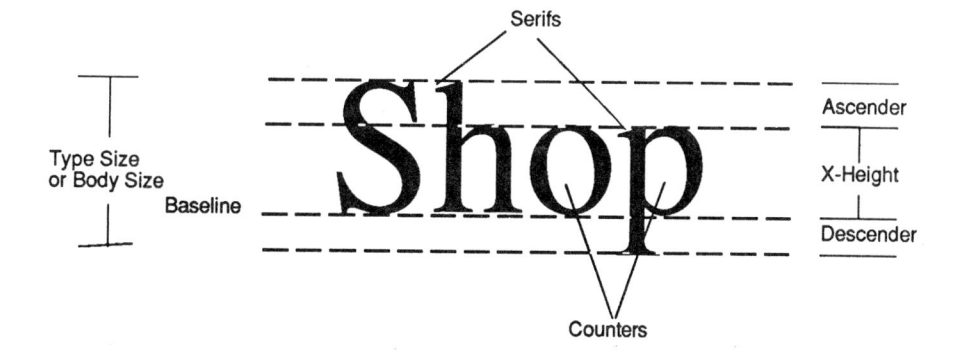

Typefaces

The art of lettering had been known long before the invention of printing in the middle of the fifteenth century. Handwritten books and manuscripts were widely known and the inscriptional characters on buildings had been used from Roman times. The increasing demand for books during the early Renaissance period ultimately led to Gutenberg's invention of movable types in 1450.

Since that time to the present day there has been a continuing process of development in letter forms and although it would be almost impossible to recognise all typefaces in use today, certain distinguishing features are recognisable, making it possible to classify them into families.

The very first types (used by Gutenberg and his contemporaries) were merely intended as imitations of the well known handwritten manuscripts. The following examples show how close the resemblance was:

**Handwritten Manuscript
15th century**

**Part of Gutenberg's
42 line Bible**

These types because of their condensed, heavy nature became known as Black Letter. There are still examples of Black Letter in use today, e.g. Old English Text.

The first types designed specifically for printing were probably the work of Nicholas Jensen in Venice around 1470. Jensen brought to the craft his skill as a master engraver and his letter forms were very different from Black Letter. The clean open lines of Jensen's type led typographers to refer to it as 'white' letter - in contrast to those of Gutenberg and his contemporaries. These new types were the first of a long, continuing series known as Roman types. There have been many changes in Roman types over the centuries so that we may now subdivide them into smaller families, each one having its own characteristics.

The characteristics by which a type may be classified are: stress, serif shape and contrast.

Stress
Refers to the distribution of thickness of the strokes of the letter and can be either (a) Diagonal or Oblique; (b) Vertical or (c) Absent - thereby giving even weight to all parts of the letter

abcdefgh
Oblique stress

four
Vertical stress

high
No stress

Serifs
These are small terminal strokes at the ends of the letter strokes and can take a number of forms:

ABCD
Bracketed

ABCD
Slab

in
Unbracketed (fine line)

Work
Unbracketed (block)

The
Sans serif (without serifs)

Contrast
Refers to the relative thicknesses of main lines of the letter.

hours
Maximum contrast

lmno
Little contrast

In attempting to classify Roman types into sub-families the above features are noted and the presence of these characteristics can fairly accurately fix its period of development.

The types of Jensen, and his contemporaries such as Aldus Manutius, became known as:

Venetians (Humanist)

abcdefghjlmnop
ABCDEFGHK

These had oblique stress, bracketed and even sometimes slab serifs and not much contrast between main and hair lines. Other distinguishing features include the sloping cross bar on the lower case 'e'.

Old Faces (Garalde)
These types originated during the sixteenth century and probably in France by Claude Garamond.

abcdefghjkm
abcdefghjklmnop
ABDFGHJ

The slab serifs on the capitals are abandoned, the capitals reduced in size, being lower than the tops of the ascenders on the lower case. The cross bar of the lower case 'e' becomes horizontal, the serifs become lighter and the contrast between main and hair lines are a little more pronounced. Stress generally is oblique.

Transitionals
These appeared during the eighteenth century and are typified by the well-known face Baskerville.

abcdefghjklmqrst

abcdefghjkmopqrstu

ABCDEHKMN

Transitional types, as the name implies, represent a period of development between the Old Faces, still largely influenced by calligraphic styles, and those called Moderns which were clearly influenced by the then new mechanical precision of industrialisation. Transitionals show a distinct flattening of the serifs; stress which is much more vertical than oblique; and a movement towards greater contrast in the main and hair lines.

Moderns (Didone)
These types are typical of the machine age and appear to be another logical step in the change towards a geometrically designed type. The most widely used is Bodoni.

abcdefghjkmorst

abdefghijkmopq

ABCDEHIJKLM

The serifs are flat, unbracketed and very fine, the stress is completely vertical and there is maximum contrast between main and hair lines. The width of the capitals is regularised in such things as a narrow 'H' and 'M' and a wide 'E'.

Egyptians and Sans Serifs

are products of the Industrial Revolution and are examples of utilitarianism. There is no contrast, no stress and in the case of the Sans Serifs, no serifs either. The serifs of the Egyptians are blocked and have equal weight with the other lines. Many variations of Sans Serif types were produced but probably best known is Univers.

abcdefghijklmnop
abcdefghijklmnop
ABCDEFGHIJKLM

A typical Egyptian is Rockwell:

adefghijkm
ABDEGHJK

Twentieth Century Romans

Are not generally modelled on earlier Romans but owe their inspiration to earlier inscriptional types. Typical in this is Perpetua, which was strongly influenced by the lettering on the Trajan Column in Rome (A.D. 113).

abcdefghijklmnop

abcdefghjklmnopqrs

ABCDEFGHIJKL

Display Types
These constitute the widest variety of designs and are intended to be used discreetly and tastefully to attract attention and not en masse. It was their misuse during the Industrial Revolution which accounted for much of that period's very poor typography. The following are just a very few of the hundreds of different ones:

GALLIA
HADRIANO STONECUT
Outline Gothic Condensed
SANS SERIF SHADED
STENCIL BOLD
DAVIDA BOLD
FONTANESI

abcdefhnt
ABCDGIQ

Fat Faces
These are exaggerated type forms and intended for use as display types. Typical is Braggadocio.

Non Roman Types
In recent years type designers have developed special letter forms for printing languages outside Europe and of the many a few are:

مختصون باللغة

Arabic

Ὁ Ὀδυσσεὺς καὶ οἱ σύντροφοι αὐτοῦ ἐμβ

Greek

ובדבר הזה אין חנו נבדלגם
מכל החי, מכל נפש ומכל

Hebrew

Все эти условия есть на некоторых

Russian

Script types
These follow closely handwriting styles. The letters should join up to one another, which is a feature of a true script face.

Type with quad

Justification styles

Justification is the technique of making all the lines in a piece of text setting the same length, whilst ensuring that all the inter-word spaces in any one line are equal.

In modern typesetting this is controlled by the computer and once the operator has indicated the line length and type size, the appropriate inter-word spaces are automatically inserted to ensure that the type fits the line length.

An example of a piece of justified setting is as follows:

The art of lettering had been known long before the invention of printing in the middle of the fifteenth century. Handwritten books and manuscripts were widely known and the inscriptional characters on buildings had been used from Roman times. The increasing demand for books during the early Renaissance period ultimately led to Gutenberg's invention of movable types in 1450. Since that time to the present day there has been a continuing process of development in letter forms and although it would be almost impossible to recognise all typefaces in use today, certain distinguishing features are recognisable, making it possible to classify them into families.

There are, however, variations to this arrangement, which in certain contexts give a pleasing result to a design. These variations are sometimes referred to as 'unjustified' setting and may take one of three forms: ranged left; ranged right; or centred.

The main advantage of these styles is that all inter-word spaces in all lines are equal to one another, giving an even density of colour to the appearance of the page and avoiding ugly gaps or 'rivers' where wide spaces appear close together.

In making all the inter-word spaces equal, it means that the lines will be of unequal length.

But, as the names of these styles imply, it is the ends of the lines which may be aligned vertically, giving the following effects:

Ranged Left

The art of lettering had been known long before the invention of printing in the middle of the fifteenth century. Handwritten books and manuscripts were widely known and the inscriptional characters on buildings had been used from Roman times. The increasing demand for books during the early Renaissance period ultimately led to Gutenberg's invention of movable types in 1450. Since that time to the present day there has been a continuing process of development in letter forms and although it would be almost impossible to recognise all typefaces in use today, certain distinguishing

Ranged Right

The art of lettering had been known long before the invention of printing in the middle of the fifteenth century. Handwritten books and manuscripts were widely known and the inscriptional characters on buildings had been used from Roman times. The increasing demand for books during the early Renaissance period ultimately led to Gutenberg's invention of movable types in 1450. Since that time to the present day there has been a continuing process of development in letter forms and although it would be almost impossible to recognise all typefaces in use today, certain distinguishing

Centred

The art of lettering had been known long before the invention of printing in the middle of the fifteenth century. Handwritten books and manuscripts were widely known and the inscriptional characters on buildings had been used from Roman times. The increasing demand for books during the early Renaissance period ultimately led to Gutenberg's invention of movable types in 1450. Since that time to the present day there has been a continuing process of development in letter forms and although it would be almost impossible to recognise all typefaces in use today, certain distinguishing features are recognisable, making it possible to classify them into families.

Indenting styles

An indent is a space left at the start of a line, usually for the purpose of beginning a new paragraph. It emanated from the days when printers left gaps at the beginning of paragraphs so that decorative initials could be drawn on the page of otherwise printed material.

Variations in the use of the indent can give different design effects to a piece of text setting.

The conventional indent is used with text matter that is justified and generally works well in this way. It is, most commonly, a space equal in width to the depth of the type size being used. This derives from the former days when typesetting in metal, where a space of this nature was called an 'em quad' – a square space. Sometimes indents were multiples of this 'quad'.

When using conventional indents, they are not usually employed on first paragraphs or on those following a heading or subhead.

Conventional Indent

A great assistance to the smooth running of the schedule is the correct and accurate marking up of copy. When properly done, it will eliminate the need for queries, which can be time consuming and costly.

An editor should strive always to anticipate queries and so mark up the copy to make it clear and unambiguous.

Composition is a costly process and anything which limits the time spent on it is to be encouraged. Typesetters welcome well-prepared copy because they can interpret the clear and precise instructions with confidence.

With unjustified setting (especially when Ranged Left) the conventional indent can give an unnecessarily ragged look to the text and it is better, therefore, not to use it in that case. However, to make paragraphs more distinct it is advisable to introduce extra space between them.

Ranged Left with Indents (not recommended)

A great assistance to the smooth running of the schedule is the correct and accurate marking up of copy. When properly done, it will eliminate the need for queries, which can be time consuming and costly.

An editor should strive always to anticipate queries and so mark up the copy to make it clear and unambiguous.

Composition is a costly process and anything which limits the time spent on it is to be encouraged. Typesetters welcome well-prepared copy because they can interpret the clear and precise instructions with confidence.

Ranged Left without Indents

A great assistance to the smooth running of the schedule is the correct and accurate marking up of copy. When properly done, it will eliminate the need for queries, which can be time consuming and costly.

An editor should strive always to anticipate queries and so mark up the copy to make it clear and unambiguous.

Composition is a costly process and anything which limits the time spent on it is to be encouraged. Typesetters welcome well-prepared copy because they can interpret the clear and precise instructions with confidence.

Hanging Indent

Is really the opposite of conventional indenting in that it is the first line which is full out and the subsequent ones which are indented. This technique is often used as a method of emphasising particular portions of copy. Variations of the hanging indent style may include bold subheads or 'bullets'.

Bold Subhead

A great assistance to the smooth running of the schedule is the correct and accurate marking up of copy. When properly done, it will eliminate the need for queries, which can be time consuming and costly.

An editor should strive always to anticipate queries and so mark up the copy to make it clear and unambiguous.

Composition is a costly process and anything which limits the time spent on it is to be encouraged. Typesetters welcome well-prepared copy because they can interpret the clear and precise instructions

With Bullets

- A great assistance to the smooth running of the schedule is the correct and accurate marking up of copy. When properly done, it will eliminate the need for queries, which can be time consuming and costly.

- An editor should strive always to anticipate queries and so mark up the copy to make it clear and unambiguous.

- Composition is a costly process and anything which limits the time spent on it is to be encouraged. Typesetters welcome well-prepared copy because they can interpret the clear and precise instructions

Letterspacing

The term 'letterspacing' means the space between letters. It can be adjusted to create the visual effect of even spacing between the letters of a word or words. This will improve the legibility and comprehension of headlines set in typefaces larger than 14 pt.

Although letterspacing is normally concerned with capital letters, lower case letters in large type sizes may also have their appearance improved by letterspacing.

To achieve visually even letterspacing, the space between some letters needs to be reduced whereas between others it may need to be increased.

On many desk top publishing systems the problem of creating visually even spacing between letters is solved automatically. Spacing is either reduced or increased to achieve a similarity between subsequent letters.

EXAMPLE

RAILWAY   RAILWAY
Bad   Good

Rules and boxes

The greater number of these devices are used to give emphasis to text and headlines and also to separate textual items. The way in which they are used depends on the type of copy and the nature of the original design and typography.

Typographical devices should be used with care and only when it enhances the text or headline(s).

There are no set rules, only general guidelines. The best examples can be found in quality magazines and newspapers, and of course, excellent examples of use of these devices can be found in many magazines, booklets, leaflets and general printed matter.

Rules

In headings rules can be used to give emphasis and strength. If the headline runs over two or three columns a rule can effectively join and unify the two elements into a coherent whole. The 'weight' or 'colour' (width or thickness in points) should not dominate the headline. Bold non-serif typefaces will require heavier rules than a light serif face.

GOOD RESPONSE AT IPEX

Big Screen Revival

or

Big Screen Revival

or

Big Screen Revival

or a box rule format

Big Screen Revival

Rules make a very effective barrier between columns of text and for separating small textual items for table work.

Warehouse Staff Grades

1. Warehouse General Manager
2. Warehouse Manager (Contracts)
3. Deputy Warehouse Manager
4. Supervisor

Boxes

A box should be the same width as a single column or a double column or a treble column. Boxes should not occupy half columns. Text columns within boxes must be set to a narrower width than column widths. Boxes within a page can be used to highlight specific articles and therefore should be given a suitable heading or sub-title. Boxes should be positioned carefully and the fewer the boxes per page the better. Full pages should not be boxed, rather use the box device to isolate or emphasise specific or important items.

The `weight' or `colour' of the box rule should conform to the overall design or `colour' of the other typographic elements in the page(s).

Schwank
Radiant Heaters

Schwank radiant heaters are particularly suitable for both local and area heating where economic factors are critical. Raidant heating is suitable for open and semi-open areas such as shopping malls, garages and offices.

GAS CENTRAL HEATING

FURTHER INFORMATION CAN BE
OBTAINED FROM

British Gas South Western

Temple Street, Keynsham, Bristol

Desktop Publishing: Design Basics

These are samples of typical rules offered on a DTP system:

Hairline ─────────────────────────────

.5pt ─────────────────────────────

1pt ─────────────────────────────

2pt ─────────────────────────────

4pt ▬▬▬▬▬▬▬▬▬▬▬▬▬▬▬▬▬

6pt ▬▬▬▬▬▬▬▬▬▬▬▬▬▬▬▬▬

8pt ▬▬▬▬▬▬▬▬▬▬▬▬▬▬▬▬▬

12pt ▬▬▬▬▬▬▬▬▬▬▬▬▬▬▬▬▬

Other options may include:

Producing a document

In order to produce a really professional looking document, it is important to take care in the preparation of the copy, the planning of the design or structure of the document, and the careful implementation of this.

The Document Structure

The structure of the text and illustrations in a document may be very simple or quite complex. Documents should be planned to look visually correct on the paper, taking into account the width of the text, the margins, the inter-column space, the readability of the type face and the type size, the amount of space between lines, and the position of various elements within the page such as illustrations.

One method often used to help to achieve these objectives is to use a basic grid for planning the document. This grid can be planned to suit various documents, and can be based upon regular or irregular columns or areas.

First of all one should determine the following:

    1. What is the document to be used for?

    2. Is it a single sheet or multiple sheets?

    3. Determine how it is going to be bound.

        a. Loose leaf ring binder

        b. Plastic comb bound

        c. Slide binder

        d. Adhesive bound

        e. Wire stitched

Whatever system is to be used, make allowance for any space required on the edge of the sheet for the method of binding to be used.

If the sheets are to be printed on one side only then they will normally be bound on the left hand edge.

If the sheets are to be printed on both sides then the pages will usually be regarded as alternatively left and right hand pages. Usually odd numbered pages are right hand pages (bound on the left), whilst even numbered pages are left hand pages (bound on the right).

We can now determine how to structure the document, and to plan the margins, column widths and the type size to be used.

If the document is to consist of a series of one sided sheets then the left and right margins will normally be equal (having allowed any additional space required for binding). The top (or head) margin would be approximately the same, but the bottom (or foot margin) needs to be slightly larger to look visually correct.

Documents printed on both sides of the sheet look best if they are designed as right and left hand pages. To look balanced and visually correct, the back margin (where it is bound) should be half of the foredge margin. A useful ratio of margins for this would be as follows:

    Back margin: 2
    Head margin: 3
    Foredge margin: 4
    Foot margin   5

Summary of structuring a document
1. Determine allowance for the binding (or punching holes)
2. Decide whether it is to be single or multiple columns
3. Establish a suitable line length
4. Prepare the margins
5. Determine a suitable type size

Desktop Publishing: Design Basics

Selection of founts

The selection or suitability of founts (or typefaces) for any given document is subject to various factors. These include:
    a. Typefaces available
    b Technical suitability
    c. Aesthetic considerations

Typefaces available

Typefaces available will vary considerably from one DTP system to another, and will be dependent on the output device that is to be used.

Type faces usually available are as follows:
    Times Roman
    Times Italic
    Times Bold
    Times Bold Italic

    Helvetica Normal
    Helvetica Oblique (Italic)
    Helvetica Bold
    Helvetica Bold Oblique (Bold Italic)

    Helvetica Narrow (Helvetica Condensed)
    Helvetica Narrow Oblique
    Helvetica Narrow Bold
    Helvetica Narrow Bold Oblique

    Avant Garde Book
    Avant Garde Book Oblique (Italic)
    Avant Garde Demi (Bold)
    Avant Garde Demi Oblique

    Palatino Roman
    Palatino Italic
    Palatino Bold
    Palatino Bold Italic

    Bookman Light
    Bookman Light Italic
    Bookman Demi (Bold)
    Bookman Demi Italic (Bold Italic)

    New Century Schoolbook Roman
    New Century Schoolbook Italic
    New Century Schoolbook Bold
    New Century Schoolbook Bold Italic

    Courier
    Courier Italic
    Courier Bold
    Courier Bold Italic

    Zapf Chancery Medium Italic
    Zapf Dingbats (symbols)

Technical suitability

The technical aspects to be considered when choosing a type face will include the readability in the environment in which the document is to be used and the paper used to print upon. Some type faces are easier to read under certain conditions, and so this may be a more important factor to consider than whether you like the appearance of the type face.

Aesthetic considerations

Very often a printed document, whether a book, magazine, sales leaflet, advertisement or almost anythingcan be assisted in conveying its message by an aesthetic or even sublimnal effect caused by the choice of a typeface and its suitability to the subject.

The following notes relate to the type faces listed earlier and suggest suitability of use.

Times Roman

Times Roman was initially designed specifically as a newspaper type face, with the requirement of good legibillityof text matter, particularly for small sizes of type. The type face has a large x-height, of medium to heavy thickness of strokes, has serifs and is slightly condensed. It has since been accepted as a very popular type face suitable for a very wide range of work such as reports, books, magazines, newsletters and all forms of commercial printing. Used in conjunction with Times Italic, Bold and Bold Italic it is a versatile type face that does not distract from the written message.

---

require high purity water to prepare ingestible medicines, disinfectant solutions, dialysis fluids, as well as for ampoule washing, etc.

Pathological Studies

Where the Pathology Department needs high purity water to feed to blood auto-analysers, liquid chromatography and atomic absorbtion detection instruments, as well as a ready source of high purity water for tissue culturing studies.

In all of these specialist areas the water needed has to be considered as a medical solution conforming to a medical prescription. This is not always easy to achieve as water supplies to hospitals and patients' homes, contain a host of impurities which, although quite suitable for drinking purposes, present a potential threat to the well-being of invalidate medical analyses.

Even in the most wholesome potable water one will find naturally occuring contaminants – such as inorganic salts, organic compounds, suspended and dissolved particles, colloidal matter and micro-organisms. In addition to these, chemicals are added to water as part of the treatment of municipal supplies. Included in this category are aluminium compounds and fluorides. A further source of contamination is the distribution pipework and storage tank through which the mains water passes and zinc, iron, copper and lead compounds will be leached into the final supply.

In the UK our supplies have been well studied and we know their natural origins to be either a lowland river source, an upland water source or an underground bore hole source. What the user does not always know is how these various sources are to be blended together to provide the continuity of supply from the Water Authority. A glance at Cambridge, London and Manchester waters *(Fig. 1)* are evidence enough of the wide range of hardness, sodium, nitrates, TDS, oxygen absorbed (the organic index), and fouling index (the colloidal indicator), levels across the country. In providing a high purity water the variation in the organic matter is always of special concern. As shown in *Fig. 2*, the seasonal variations need to be taken into account – high levels occur traditionally in early winter and low levels in summer. Therefore, before a water treatment design can be matched to the medical prescription, afull water analysis of the feed water supply must be made. A one litre sample is normally enough for our laboratory to carry this out, although the FI check can only be taken from a tap on site using a special FI Test Kit.

The proven treatment techniques traditionally offered for hospital medical applications have been – Distillation, Ion Exchange Resin Deionisation (DI) and Reverse Osmosis (RO). Each has certain advantages and disadvantages *(Fig.3)*.

Distillation is bulky and costly to both operate and maintain but it does satisfy the British Pharmacopoeia for the preparation of purogen-free water for injection.

Ion Exchange Resins are convenient to apply and the most effective in the removal of ionic contaminants but cannot be considered on their own for the removal of bacteria or low molecular weight organics.

Reverse osmosis

Reverse Osmosis, the technique where impurities are prevented from crossing a synthetic membrane barrier, is the most flexible for treating varying water supply qualities and removes bacteria, purogens, colloids and organic matter most effectively, as well as 90-95% of inorganic matter, including metallic compounds. It probably has the highest capital cost but the lowest running cost. As a result, in combination with an ion exchange resin deioniser, a high purity water can be provided at the cheapest possible cost per litre *(Fig.4)*.

A triple-pass still or an ion exchange cartridge deioniser on their own would provide a luS/cm quality water for btween 3-10 pence per litre, a combination of reverse osmosis followed by ion

Above example set in 9/10pt Times Roman

Helvetica
Helvetica is a non-seriffed type face with a large x-height that has subtle variations of stroke thickness which combine to make it a clear and precise type face to read. Despite this, non-seriffed type faces tend to be slightly harsh for the reader which suggests that it is not particularly suitable for books or very long documents. Ideal for shorter reports, technical documents, and a good general purpose type face suitable for notices, price lists and where information needs to be clear. Use in conjunction with bold, italic and bold italic for variation in emphasis.

Floppy Disk Care

Floppy disks can easily be damaged if certain precautions are not taken when handling them.

1. Do not touch the exposed areas of the disk.
2. Do not bend the disk.
3. Do not write on a label attached to a floppy disk using a ballpoint pen or pencil. Either prepare the label in advance and then attach to the disk or write on the label using a felt-tip pen.
4. Keep the disks away from direct sunlight, heat, magnetic fields or X-rays, or the data may be erased from the disk.
5. Always return the disks to their protective envelopes when not in use and place them in a drawer or plastic container or they may be accidently damaged.
6. Make a back-up of important disks, particularly if you are going to send a disk to another person or company.

Set in 10/11pt Helvetica Medium and Bold

Avant Garde Book
Many type faces in this style were influenced by the functional thoughts and designs created at the Bauhaus in Germany during the 1930's. Avant Garde is a non-seriffed geometrically proportioned type face based mainly on circles and straight lines. Since there is little subtlety in the design it is not really suitable for books or magazines unless the subject matter, such as art, design or photography, could be influenced by using this type face.

---

the art of the

escapist

edited by richard nixon

published by the watergate press

Set in Avant Garde Medium and Bold

Palatino
This type face, like Zapf Chancery, has a strong influence from the chancery cursive of the 15/16th century. It can create pleasing effects in roman, italic and bold. It may be used for a range of work from newsletters, magazines, reports and for displayed work.

> # NEW
> ## 1988
> # habitat
> ### CATALOGUE
>
> *If you thought you knew Habitat, then think again. Discover the difference in the new Habitat Catalogue, featuring a special £5 money off voucher (redeemable when you spend £50 or more). Pick up a copy at your nearest Habitat or local newsagents for just £1.95.*
>
> **Discover the difference ...**

Set in Palatino Roman, Bold and Italic

Bookman
Bookman has been designed so that can be used for a range of different kinds of work. It is easy to read, and if used with its accompanying bold, italic and bold italic, can be used to create variations of importance to the different parts of the document.

> **Chapter 6**
>
> # *Media Studies*
> ## Television
>
> This case study describes work in two schools with a CSE drama group and a sixth-form media-studies group respectively. In both cases the medium of recorded sound and vision was studied and used for its own sake, rather than to explore a traditional curriculum subject. Both teachers approached their work as a means of developing in their pupils

Set in Bookman Roman, Bold and Bold Italic

New Century Schoolbook
This type face was originally designed for the Century Magazine in 1894 and then redesigned in 1934. It has a large x-height, strong bracketed serifs that are square at the ends, with very open centres to the characters giving it very good legibility. It is probably for this reason that it is often used in books for young children.

Capital letters

Names of people start with capital letters. John and Mary are names of people. Continents start with capital letters. Africa is a continent. Names of countries also start with capital letters.

Set in 14/16pt New Century Schoolbook

Courier
Courier is a type face designed to look as if it is created on a typewriter. Ideal for circulars, letters and appeals where the publisher is trying to convey the personal touch.

The Rectory,
Little Northwick,
Northwick-in-the Marsh,
Shropshire.

```
Dear Parishioner,

   Now that you have probably just returned from your
holidays abroad, may I remind you that our appeal fund
for the restoration of the church has still not reached
its target figure.
```

This letter was set in 10/14 pt Courier Normal

Zapf Chancery Medium Italic
This type face is based upon a style of writing employed by scribes in Venice and Rome during the 15th and 16th centuries, usually referred to as a Chancery Cursive. Many other type faces, notably italics, were also derived from the same source. Although it is a beautiful type face, care must be taken in where it is used. If it is used for long passages of text it can be difficult to read. The capital letters are designed specifically as capital letters, so therefore do not set complete words or lines in capitals since the fit of the characters will be impaired, and the words will less easy to read. Typical use is for invitations, informal notices and personal letterheadings.

Captain & Mrs. Charles Bowles
request the pleasure of the company of
..
at the marriage of their daughter

Caroline
with
Robert Southey

at Holy Trinity Church, Lymington
on Saturday 12th July 1811,
and afterwards at the White Hart Inn, Boldre

Set in Zapf Chancery Medium Italic

Typeface specimen charts

The selection of suitable typefaces is a complete subject but the following points are guides.

a. Do not mix too many different founts. The end result looks more like a type specimen book than a document to be read.

b. For ease of reading of long documents, a simple serifed type face is most suitable, and does not cause the reader distractions. Italic may be used within the text to emphasise where necessary, but do not do this too frequently or it distracts too much. A bold face used for headings makes them easy to distinguish from the text matter.

c. Use non-serifed faces for clarity of technical documents or for giving impact to a message.

d. Limit the use of decorative typefaces.

On the following pages we give specimens of text and display faces as a guide to selection and casting-off.

6 point

The selection of appropriate type faces and type sizes is very important to achieve both readability and suitability for the given subject matter. If the type face chosen is unsuitable then it may detract from the message of the written word, whilst an inappropriate type size can make reading very difficult.

8 point

The selection of appropriate type faces and type sizes is very important to achieve both readability and suitability for the given subject matter. If the type face chosen is unsuitable then it may detract from the message of the written word, whilst an inappropriate type size can make reading very difficult.

9 point

The selection of appropriate type faces and type sizes is very important to achieve both readability and suitability for the given subject matter. If the type face chosen is unsuitable then it may detract from the message of the written word, whilst an inappropriate type size can make reading very difficult.

10 point

The selection of appropriate type faces and type sizes is very important to achieve both readability and suitability for the given subject matter. If the type face chosen is unsuitable then it may detract from the message of the written word, whilst an inappropriate type size can make reading very difficult.

12 point

The selection of appropriate type faces and type sizes is very important to achieve both readability and suitability for the given subject matter. If the type face chosen is unsuitable then it may detract from the message of the written word, whilst an inappropriate type size can make reading very difficult.

14 point

The selection of appropriate type faces and type sizes is very important to achieve both readability and suitability for the given subject matter. If the type face chosen is unsuitable then it may detract from the message of the written word, whilst an inappropriate type size can make reading very difficult.

PICAS

| 6 | 12 | 18 | 24 | 30 | 36 |

AVANT GARDE TEXT SIZES

Desktop Publishing: Design Basics

6 point

The selection of appropriate type faces and type sizes is very important to achieve both readability and suitability for the given subject matter. If the type face chosen is unsuitable then it may detract from the message of the written word, whilst an inappropriate type size can make reading very difficult.

8 point

The selection of appropriate type faces and type sizes is very important to achieve both readability and suitability for the given subject matter. If the type face chosen is unsuitable then it may detract from the message of the written word, whilst an inappropriate type size can make reading very difficult.

9 point

The selection of appropriate type faces and type sizes is very important to achieve both readability and suitability for the given subject matter. If the type face chosen is unsuitable then it may detract from the message of the written word, whilst an inappropriate type size can make reading very difficult.

10 point

The selection of appropriate type faces and type sizes is very important to achieve both readability and suitability for the given subject matter. If the type face chosen is unsuitable then it may detract from the message of the written word, whilst an inappropriate type size can make reading very difficult.

12 point

The selection of appropriate type faces and type sizes is very important to achieve both readability and suitability for the given subject matter. If the type face chosen is unsuitable then it may detract from the message of the written word, whilst an inappropriate type size can make reading very difficult.

14 point

The selection of appropriate type faces and type sizes is very important to achieve both readability and suitability for the given subject matter. If the type face chosen is unsuitable then it may detract from the message of the written word, whilst an inappropriate type size can make reading very difficult.

PICAS

| 6 | 12 | 18 | 24 | 30 | 36 |

BOOKMAN TEXT SIZES

6 point

The selection of appropriate type faces and type sizes is very important to achieve both readability and suitability for the given subject matter. If the type face chosen is unsuitable then it may detract from the message of the written word, whilst an inappropriate type size can make reading very difficult.

8 point

The selection of appropriate type faces and type sizes is very important to achieve both readability and suitability for the given subject matter. If the type face chosen is unsuitable then it may detract from the message of the written word, whilst an inappropriate type size can make reading very difficult.

9 point

The selection of appropriate type faces and type sizes is very important to achieve both readability and suitability for the given subject matter. If the type face chosen is unsuitable then it may detract from the message of the written word, whilst an inappropriate type size can make reading very difficult.

10 point

The selection of appropriate type faces and type sizes is very important to achieve both readability and suitability for the given subject matter. If the type face chosen is unsuitable then it may detract from the message of the written word, whilst an inappropriate type size can make reading very difficult.

12 point

The selection of appropriate type faces and type sizes is very important to achieve both readability and suitability for the given subject matter. If the type face chosen is unsuitable then it may detract from the message of the written word, whilst an inappropriate type size can make reading very difficult.

14 point

The selection of appropriate type faces and type sizes is very important to achieve both readability and suitability for the given subject matter. If the type face chosen is unsuitable then it may detract from the message of the written word, whilst an inappropriate type size can make reading very difficult.

PICAS

| 6 | 12 | 18 | 24 | 30 | 36 |

HELVETICA TEXT SIZES

6 point

The selection of appropriate type faces and type sizes is very important to achieve both readability and suitability for the given subject matter. If the type face chosen is unsuitable then it may detract from the message of the written word, whilst an inappropriate type size can make reading very difficult.

8 point

The selection of appropriate type faces and type sizes is very important to achieve both readability and suitability for the given subject matter. If the type face chosen is unsuitable then it may detract from the message of the written word, whilst an inappropriate type size can make reading very difficult.

9 point

The selection of appropriate type faces and type sizes is very important to achieve both readability and suitability for the given subject matter. If the type face chosen is unsuitable then it may detract from the message of the written word, whilst an inappropriate type size can make reading very difficult.

10 point

The selection of appropriate type faces and type sizes is very important to achieve both readability and suitability for the given subject matter. If the type face chosen is unsuitable then it may detract from the message of the written word, whilst an inappropriate type size can make reading very difficult.

12 point

The selection of appropriate type faces and type sizes is very important to achieve both readability and suitability for the given subject matter. If the type face chosen is unsuitable then it may detract from the message of the written word, whilst an inappropriate type size can make reading very difficult.

14 point

The selection of appropriate type faces and type sizes is very important to achieve both readability and suitability for the given subject matter. If the type face chosen is unsuitable then it may detract from the message of the written word, whilst an inappropriate type size can make reading very difficult.

PICAS

| 6 | 12 | 18 | 24 | 30 | 36 |

NEW CENTURY SCHOOLBOOK TEXT SIZES

6 point

The selection of appropriate type faces and type sizes is very important to achieve both readability and suitability for the given subject matter. If the type face chosen is unsuitable then it may detract from the message of the written word, whilst an inappropriate type size can make reading very difficult.

8 point

The selection of appropriate type faces and type sizes is very important to achieve both readability and suitability for the given subject matter. If the type face chosen is unsuitable then it may detract from the message of the written word, whilst an inappropriate type size can make reading very difficult.

9 point

The selection of appropriate type faces and type sizes is very important to achieve both readability and suitability for the given subject matter. If the type face chosen is unsuitable then it may detract from the message of the written word, whilst an inappropriate type size can make reading very difficult.

10 point

The selection of appropriate type faces and type sizes is very important to achieve both readability and suitability for the given subject matter. If the type face chosen is unsuitable then it may detract from the message of the written word, whilst an inappropriate type size can make reading very difficult.

12 point

The selection of appropriate type faces and type sizes is very important to achieve both readability and suitability for the given subject matter. If the type face chosen is unsuitable then it may detract from the message of the written word, whilst an inappropriate type size can make reading very difficult.

14 point

The selection of appropriate type faces and type sizes is very important to achieve both readability and suitability for the given subject matter. If the type face chosen is unsuitable then it may detract from the message of the written word, whilst an inappropriate type size can make reading very difficult.

PICAS

| 6 | 12 | 18 | 24 | 30 | 36 |

PALATINO TEXT SIZES

Desktop Publishing: Design Basics

6 point

The selection of appropriate type faces and type sizes is very important to achieve both readability and suitability for the given subject matter. If the type face chosen is unsuitable then it may detract from the message of the written word, whilst an inappropriate type size can make reading very difficult.

8 point

The selection of appropriate type faces and type sizes is very important to achieve both readability and suitability for the given subject matter. If the type face chosen is unsuitable then it may detract from the message of the written word, whilst an inappropriate type size can make reading very difficult.

9 point

The selection of appropriate type faces and type sizes is very important to achieve both readability and suitability for the given subject matter. If the type face chosen is unsuitable then it may detract from the message of the written word, whilst an inappropriate type size can make reading very difficult.

10 point

The selection of appropriate type faces and type sizes is very important to achieve both readability and suitability for the given subject matter. If the type face chosen is unsuitable then it may detract from the message of the written word, whilst an inappropriate type size can make reading very difficult.

12 point

The selection of appropriate type faces and type sizes is very important to achieve both readability and suitability for the given subject matter. If the type face chosen is unsuitable then it may detract from the message of the written word, whilst an inappropriate type size can make reading very difficult.

14 point

The selection of appropriate type faces and type sizes is very important to achieve both readability and suitability for the given subject matter. If the type face chosen is unsuitable then it may detract from the message of the written word, whilst an inappropriate type size can make reading very difficult.

PICAS

| 6 | 12 | 18 | 24 | 30 | 36 |

TIMES TEXT SIZES

14 point

ABCDEFGHIJKLMNOPQRSTUVWXYZ
abcdefghijklmnopqrstuvwxyz

18 point

ABCDEFGHIJKLMNOPQRSTUVWXYZ
abcdefghijklmnopqrstuvwxyz

24 point

ABCDEFGHIJKLMNOPQRSTUVWXYZ
abcdefghijklmnopqrstuvwxyz

30 point

ABCDEFGHIJKLMNOPQRSTUVWXYZ
abcdefghijklmnopqrstuvwxyz

36 point

ABCDEFGHIJKLMNOPQRS
abcdefghijklmnopqrstuvw

PICAS

| 6 | 12 | 18 | 24 | 30 | 36 |

AVANT GARDE DEMI

Desktop Publishing: Design Basics

48 point

ABCDEFGHIJKLMNO
abcdefghijklmnop

60 point

ABCDEFGHIJKL
abcdefghijklm

72 point

ABCDEFGHIJ
abcdefghijk

PICAS

| 6 | 12 | 18 | 24 | 30 | 36 |

AVANT GARDE DEMI

14 point

ABCDEFGHIJKLMNOPQRSTUVWXYZ
abcdefghijklmnopqrstuvwxyz

18 point

ABCDEFGHIJKLMNOPQRSTUVWXYZ
abcdefghijklmnopqrstuvwxyz

24 point

ABCDEFGHIJKLMNOPQRSTUVWXYZ
abcdefghijklmnopqrstuvwxyz

30 point

ABCDEFGHIJKLMNOPQRSTUVWXYZ
abcdefghijklmnopqrstuvwxyz

36 point

ABCDEFGHIJKLMNOPQRS
abcdefghijklmnopqrstuvw

PICAS | 6 | 12 | 18 | 24 | 30 | 36

AVANT GARDE

Desktop Publishing: Design Basics

48 point

ABCDEFGHIJKLMNO
abcdefghijklmnop

60 point

ABCDEFGHIJKL
abcdefghijklm

72 point

ABCDEFGHIJ
abcdefghijk

PICAS

| 6 | 12 | 18 | 24 | 30 | 36 |

AVANT GARDE

14 point

ABCDEFGHIJKLMNOPQRSTUVWXYZ
abcdefghijklmnopqrstuvwxyz

18 point

ABCDEFGHIJKLMNOPQRSTUVWXYZ
abcdefghijklmnopqrstuvwxyz

24 point

ABCDEFGHIJKLMNOPQRSTUVWXYZ
abcdefghijklmnopqrstuvwxyz

30 point

ABCDEFGHIJKLMNOPQRSTUVWXYZ
abcdefghijklmnopqrstuvwxyz

36 point

ABCDEFGHIJKLMNOPQRS
abcdefghijklmnopqrstuvw

PICAS

| 6 | 12 | 18 | 24 | 30 | 36 |

AVANT GARDE ITALIC

Desktop Publishing: Design Basics

48 point

ABCDEFGHIJKLMNO
abcdefghijklmnop

60 point

ABCDEFGHIJKL
abcdefghijklm

72 point

ABCDEFGHIJ
abcdefghijk

PICAS

| 6 | 12 | 18 | 24 | 30 | 36 |

AVANT GARDE ITALIC

14 point

ABCDEFGHIJKLMNOPQRSTUVWXYZ
abcdefghijklmnopqrstuvwxyz

18 point

ABCDEFGHIJKLMNOPQRSTUVWXYZ
abcdefghijklmnopqrstuvwxyz

24 point

ABCDEFGHIJKLMNOPQRSTUVWXYZ
abcdefghijklmnopqrstuvwxyz

30 point

ABCDEFGHIJKLMNOPQRSTUVWXYZ
abcdefghijklmnopqrstuvwxyz

36 point

ABCDEFGHIJKLMNOPQRS
abcdefghijklmnopqrstuvw

PICAS

| 6 | 12 | 18 | 24 | 30 | 36 |

AVANT GARDE DEMI ITALIC

48 point

ABCDEFGHIJKLMNO
abcdefghijklmnop

60 point

ABCDEFGHIJKL
abcdefghijklm

72 point

ABCDEFGHIJ
abcdefghijk

PICAS

| 6 | 12 | 18 | 24 | 30 | 36 |

AVANT GARDE DEMI ITALIC

14 point

ABCDEFGHIJKLMNOPQRSTUVWXYZ
abcdefghijklmnopqrstuvwxyz

18 point

ABCDEFGHIJKLMNOPQRSTUVWXYZ
abcdefghijklmnopqrstuvwxyz

24 point

ABCDEFGHIJKLMNOPQRSTUVWXYZ
abcdefghijklmnopqrstuvwxyz

30 point

ABCDEFGHIJKLMNOPQRSTUVWXYZ
abcdefghijklmnopqrstuvwxyz

36 point

ABCDEFGHIJKLMNOPQRS
abcdefghijklmnopqrstuvw

PICAS

| 6 | 12 | 18 | 24 | 30 | 36 |

BOOKMAN

48 point

ABCDEFGHIJKLMNO
abcdefghijklmnop

60 point

ABCDEFGHIJKL
abcdefghijklm

72 point

ABCDEFGHIJ
abcdefghijk

PICAS

| 6 | 12 | 18 | 24 | 30 | 36 |

BOOKMAN

14 point

ABCDEFGHIJKLMNOPQRSTUVWXYZ
abcdefghijklmnopqrstuvwxyz

18 point

ABCDEFGHIJKLMNOPQRSTUVWXYZ
abcdefghijklmnopqrstuvwxyz

24 point

ABCDEFGHIJKLMNOPQRSTUVWXYZ
abcdefghijklmnopqrstuvwxyz

30 point

ABCDEFGHIJKLMNOPQRSTUVWXYZ
abcdefghijklmnopqrstuvwxyz

36 point

ABCDEFGHIJKLMNOPQRS
abcdefghijklmnopqrstuvw

PICAS

| 6 | 12 | 18 | 24 | 30 | 36 |

BOOKMAN DEMI

Desktop Publishing: Design Basics

48 point

ABCDEFGHIJKLMNO
abcdefghijklmnop

60 point

ABCDEFGHIJKL
abcdefghijklm

72 point

ABCDEFGHIJ
abcdefghijk

PICAS

| 6 | 12 | 18 | 24 | 30 | 36 |

BOOKMAN DEMI

14 point

ABCDEFGHIJKLMNOPQRSTUVWXYZ
abcdefghijklmnopqrstuvwxyz

18 point

ABCDEFGHIJKLMNOPQRSTUVWXYZ
abcdefghijklmnopqrstuvwxyz

24 point

ABCDEFGHIJKLMNOPQRSTUVWXYZ
abcdefghijklmnopqrstuvwxyz

30 point

ABCDEFGHIJKLMNOPQRSTUVWXYZ
abcdefghijklmnopqrstuvwxyz

36 point

ABCDEFGHIJKLMNOPQRS
abcdefghijklmnopqrstuvw

PICAS

| 6 | 12 | 18 | 24 | 30 | 36 |

BOOKMAN LIGHT ITALIC

Desktop Publishing: Design Basics

48 point

ABCDEFGHIJKLMNO
abcdefghijklmnop

60 point

ABCDEFGHIJKL
abcdefghijklm

72 point

ABCDEFGHIJ
abcdefghijk

PICAS

| 6 | 12 | 18 | 24 | 30 | 36 |

BOOKMAN LIGHT ITALIC

14 point

ABCDEFGHIJKLMNOPQRSTUVWXYZ
abcdefghijklmnopqrstuvwxyz

18 point

ABCDEFGHIJKLMNOPQRSTUVWXYZ
abcdefghijklmnopqrstuvwxyz

24 point

ABCDEFGHIJKLMNOPQRSTUVWXYZ
abcdefghijklmnopqrstuvwxyz

30 point

ABCDEFGHIJKLMNOPQRSTUVWXYZ
abcdefghijklmnopqrstuvwxyz

36 point

ABCDEFGHIJKLMNOPQRS
abcdefghijklmnopqrstuvw

PICAS

	6	12	18	24	30	36

BOOKMAN DEMI ITALIC

Desktop Publishing: Design Basics

48 point

ABCDEFGHIJKLMNO
abcdefghijklmnop

60 point

ABCDEFGHIJKL
abcdefghijklm

72 point

ABCDEFGHIJ
abcdefghijk

PICAS | 6 | 12 | 18 | 24 | 30 | 36

BOOKMAN DEMI ITALIC

14 point

ABCDEFGHIJKLMNOPQRSTUVWXYZ
abcdefghijklmnopqrstuvwxyz

18 point

ABCDEFGHIJKLMNOPQRSTUVWXYZ
abcdefghijklmnopqrstuvwxyz

24 point

ABCDEFGHIJKLMNOPQRSTUVWXYZ
abcdefghijklmnopqrstuvwxyz

30 point

ABCDEFGHIJKLMNOPQRSTUVWXYZ
abcdefghijklmnopqrstuvwxyz

36 point

ABCDEFGHIJKLMNOPQRS
abcdefghijklmnopqrstuvw

PICAS | 6 | 12 | 18 | 24 | 30 | 36

HELVETICA

Desktop Publishing: Design Basics

48 point

ABCDEFGHIJKLMNO
abcdefghijklmnop

60 point

ABCDEFGHIJKL
abcdefghijklm

72 point

ABCDEFGHIJ
abcdefghijk

PICAS

| | 6 | 12 | 18 | 24 | 30 | 36 |

HELVETICA

14 point

ABCDEFGHIJKLMNOPQRSTUVWXYZ
abcdefghijklmnopqrstuvwxyz

18 point

ABCDEFGHIJKLMNOPQRSTUVWXYZ
abcdefghijklmnopqrstuvwxyz

24 point

ABCDEFGHIJKLMNOPQRSTUVWXYZ
abcdefghijklmnopqrstuvwxyz

30 point

ABCDEFGHIJKLMNOPQRSTUVWXYZ
abcdefghijklmnopqrstuvwxyz

36 point

ABCDEFGHIJKLMNOPQRS
abcdefghijklmnopqrstuvw

PICAS

| 6 | 12 | 18 | 24 | 30 | 36 |

HELVETICA BOLD

Desktop Publishing: Design Basics

48 point

ABCDEFGHIJKLMNO
abcdefghijklmnop

60 point

ABCDEFGHIJKL
abcdefghijklm

72 point

ABCDEFGHIJ
abcdefghijk

PICAS

| 6 | 12 | 18 | 24 | 30 | 36 |

HELVETICA BOLD

14 point

ABCDEFGHIJKLMNOPQRSTUVWXYZ
abcdefghijklmnopqrstuvwxyz

18 point

ABCDEFGHIJKLMNOPQRSTUVWXYZ
abcdefghijklmnopqrstuvwxyz

24 point

ABCDEFGHIJKLMNOPQRSTUVWXYZ
abcdefghijklmnopqrstuvwxyz

30 point

ABCDEFGHIJKLMNOPQRSTUVWXYZ
abcdefghijklmnopqrstuvwxyz

36 point

ABCDEFGHIJKLMNOPQRS
abcdefghijklmnopqrstuvw

PICAS

| 6 | 12 | 18 | 24 | 30 | 36 |

HELVETICA ITALIC

Desktop Publishing: Design Basics

48 point

ABCDEFGHIJKLMNO
abcdefghijklmnop

60 point

ABCDEFGHIJKL
abcdefghijklm

72 point

ABCDEFGHIJ
abcdefghijk

PICAS

| 6 | 12 | 18 | 24 | 30 | 36 |

HELVETICA ITALIC

14 point

ABCDEFGHIJKLMNOPQRSTUVWXYZ
abcdefghijklmnopqrstuvwxyz

18 point

ABCDEFGHIJKLMNOPQRSTUVWXYZ
abcdefghijklmnopqrstuvwxyz

24 point

ABCDEFGHIJKLMNOPQRSTUVWXYZ
abcdefghijklmnopqrstuvwxyz

30 point

ABCDEFGHIJKLMNOPQRSTUVWXYZ
abcdefghijklmnopqrstuvwxyz

36 point

ABCDEFGHIJKLMNOPQRS
abcdefghijklmnopqrstuvw

PICAS

| | 6 | 12 | 18 | 24 | 30 | 36 |

HELVETICA BOLD ITALIC

Desktop Publishing: Design Basics

48 point

ABCDEFGHIJKLMNO
abcdefghijklmnop

60 point

ABCDEFGHIJKL
abcdefghijklm

72 point

ABCDEFGHIJ
abcdefghijk

PICAS

| 6 | 12 | 18 | 24 | 30 | 36 |

HELVETICA BOLD ITALIC

14 point

ABCDEFGHIJKLMNOPQRSTUVWXYZ
abcdefghijklmnopqrstuvwxyz

18 point

ABCDEFGHIJKLMNOPQRSTUVWXYZ
abcdefghijklmnopqrstuvwxyz

24 point

ABCDEFGHIJKLMNOPQRSTUVWXYZ
abcdefghijklmnopqrstuvwxyz

30 point

ABCDEFGHIJKLMNOPQRSTUVWXYZ
abcdefghijklmnopqrstuvwxyz

36 point

ABCDEFGHIJKLMNOPQRS
abcdefghijklmnopqrstuvw

PICAS | 6 | 12 | 18 | 24 | 30 | 36

HELVETICA CONDENSED

Desktop Publishing: Design Basics

48 point

ABCDEFGHIJKLMNO
abcdefghijklmnop

60 point

ABCDEFGHIJKL
abcdefghijklm

72 point

ABCDEFGHIJ
abcdefghijk

PICAS | 6 | 12 | 18 | 24 | 30 | 36

HELVETICA CONDENSED

14 point

ABCDEFGHIJKLMNOPQRSTUVWXYZ
abcdefghijklmnopqrstuvwxyz

18 point

ABCDEFGHIJKLMNOPQRSTUVWXYZ
abcdefghijklmnopqrstuvwxyz

24 point

ABCDEFGHIJKLMNOPQRSTUVWXYZ
abcdefghijklmnopqrstuvwxyz

30 point

ABCDEFGHIJKLMNOPQRSTUVWXYZ
abcdefghijklmnopqrstuvwxyz

36 point

ABCDEFGHIJKLMNOPQRS
abcdefghijklmnopqrstuvw

PICAS | 6 | 12 | 18 | 24 | 30 | 36

HELVETICA BOLD CONDENSED

Desktop Publishing: Design Basics

48 point

ABCDEFGHIJKLMNO
abcdefghijklmnop

60 point

ABCDEFGHIJKL
abcdefghijklm

72 point

ABCDEFGHIJ
abcdefghijk

PICAS

| 6 | 12 | 18 | 24 | 30 | 36 |

HELVETICA BOLD CONDENSED

14 point

ABCDEFGHIJKLMNOPQRSTUVWXYZ
abcdefghijklmnopqrstuvwxyz

18 point

ABCDEFGHIJKLMNOPQRSTUVWXYZ
abcdefghijklmnopqrstuvwxyz

24 point

ABCDEFGHIJKLMNOPQRSTUVWXYZ
abcdefghijklmnopqrstuvwxyz

30 point

ABCDEFGHIJKLMNOPQRSTUVWXYZ
abcdefghijklmnopqrstuvwxyz

36 point

ABCDEFGHIJKLMNOPQRS
abcdefghijklmnopqrstuvw

PICAS
| 6 | 12 | 18 | 24 | 30 | 36 |

HELVETICA CONDENSED ITALIC

Desktop Publishing: Design Basics

48 point

ABCDEFGHIJKLMNO
abcdefghijklmnop

60 point

ABCDEFGHIJKL
abcdefghijklm

72 point

ABCDEFGHIJ
abcdefghijk

PICAS

| 6 | 12 | 18 | 24 | 30 | 36 |

HELVETICA CONDENSED ITALIC

14 point

ABCDEFGHIJKLMNOPQRSTUVWXYZ
abcdefghijklmnopqrstuvwxyz

18 point

ABCDEFGHIJKLMNOPQRSTUVWXYZ
abcdefghijklmnopqrstuvwxyz

24 point

ABCDEFGHIJKLMNOPQRSTUVWXYZ
abcdefghijklmnopqrstuvwxyz

30 point

ABCDEFGHIJKLMNOPQRSTUVWXYZ
abcdefghijklmnopqrstuvwxyz

36 point

ABCDEFGHIJKLMNOPQRS
abcdefghijklmnopqrstuvw

PICAS

| 6 | 12 | 18 | 24 | 30 | 36 |

HELVETICA BOLD CONDENSED ITALIC

Desktop Publishing: Design Basics

48 point

ABCDEFGHIJKLMNO
abcdefghijklmnop

60 point

ABCDEFGHIJKL
abcdefghijklm

72 point

ABCDEFGHIJ
abcdefghijk

PICAS | 6 | 12 | 18 | 24 | 30 | 36

HELVETICA BOLD CONDENSED ITALIC

14 point

ABCDEFGHIJKLMNOPQRSTUVWXYZ
abcdefghijklmnopqrstuvwxyz

18 point

ABCDEFGHIJKLMNOPQRSTUVWXYZ
abcdefghijklmnopqrstuvwxyz

24 point

ABCDEFGHIJKLMNOPQRSTUVWXYZ
abcdefghijklmnopqrstuvwxyz

30 point

ABCDEFGHIJKLMNOPQRSTUVWXYZ
abcdefghijklmnopqrstuvwxyz

36 point

ABCDEFGHIJKLMNOPQRS
abcdefghijklmnopqrstuvw

PICAS
| 6 | 12 | 18 | 24 | 30 | 36 |

NEW CENTURY SCHOOLBOOK

48 point

ABCDEFGHIJKLMNO
abcdefghijklmnop

60 point

ABCDEFGHIJKL
abcdefghijklm

72 point

ABCDEFGHIJ
abcdefghijk

PICAS
| 6 | 12 | 18 | 24 | 30 | 36 |

NEW CENTURY SCHOOLBOOK

14 point

ABCDEFGHIJKLMNOPQRSTUVWXYZ
abcdefghijklmnopqrstuvwxyz

18 point

ABCDEFGHIJKLMNOPQRSTUVWXYZ
abcdefghijklmnopqrstuvwxyz

24 point

ABCDEFGHIJKLMNOPQRSTUVWXYZ
abcdefghijklmnopqrstuvwxyz

30 point

ABCDEFGHIJKLMNOPQRSTUVWXYZ
abcdefghijklmnopqrstuvwxyz

36 point

ABCDEFGHIJKLMNOPQRS
abcdefghijklmnopqrstuvw

PICAS | 6 | 12 | 18 | 24 | 30 | 36

NEW CENTURY SCHOOLBOOK BOLD

Desktop Publishing: Design Basics

48 point

ABCDEFGHIJKLMNO
abcdefghijklmnop

60 point

ABCDEFGHIJKL
abcdefghijklm

72 point

ABCDEFGHIJ
abcdefghijk

PICAS
| 6 | 12 | 18 | 24 | 30 | 36 |

NEW CENTURY SCHOOLBOOK BOLD

14 point

ABCDEFGHIJKLMNOPQRSTUVWXYZ
abcdefghijklmnopqrstuvwxyz

18 point

ABCDEFGHIJKLMNOPQRSTUVWXYZ
abcdefghijklmnopqrstuvwxyz

24 point

ABCDEFGHIJKLMNOPQRSTUVWXYZ
abcdefghijklmnopqrstuvwxyz

30 point

ABCDEFGHIJKLMNOPQRSTUVWXYZ
abcdefghijklmnopqrstuvwxyz

36 point

ABCDEFGHIJKLMNOPQRS
abcdefghijklmnopqrstuvw

PICAS
| 6 | 12 | 18 | 24 | 30 | 36 |

NEW CENTURY SCHOOLBOOK BOLD ITALIC

Desktop Publishing: Design Basics

48 point

ABCDEFGHIJKLMNO
abcdefghijklmnop

60 point

ABCDEFGHIJKL
abcdefghijklm

72 point

ABCDEFGHIJ
abcdefghijk

PICAS

| 6 | 12 | 18 | 24 | 30 | 36 |

NEW CENTURY SCHOOLBOOK BOLD ITALIC

14 point

ABCDEFGHIJKLMNOPQRSTUVWXYZ
abcdefghijklmnopqrstuvwxyz

18 point

ABCDEFGHIJKLMNOPQRSTUVWXYZ
abcdefghijklmnopqrstuvwxyz

24 point

ABCDEFGHIJKLMNOPQRSTUVWXYZ
abcdefghijklmnopqrstuvwxyz

30 point

ABCDEFGHIJKLMNOPQRSTUVWXYZ
abcdefghijklmnopqrstuvwxyz

36 point

ABCDEFGHIJKLMNOPQRS
abcdefghijklmnopqrstuvw

PICAS
| | 6 | 12 | 18 | 24 | 30 | 36 |

NEW CENTURY SCHOOLBOOK ITALIC

48 point

ABCDEFGHIJKLMNO
abcdefghijklmnop

60 point

ABCDEFGHIJKL
abcdefghijklm

72 point

ABCDEFGHIJ
abcdefghijk

PICAS

| 6 | 12 | 18 | 24 | 30 | 36 |

NEW CENTURY SCHOOLBOOK ITALIC

14 point

ABCDEFGHIJKLMNOPQRSTUVWXYZ
abcdefghijklmnopqrstuvwxyz

18 point

ABCDEFGHIJKLMNOPQRSTUVWXYZ
abcdefghijklmnopqrstuvwxyz

24 point

ABCDEFGHIJKLMNOPQRSTUVWXYZ
abcdefghijklmnopqrstuvwxyz

30 point

ABCDEFGHIJKLMNOPQRSTUVWXYZ
abcdefghijklmnopqrstuvwxyz

36 point

ABCDEFGHIJKLMNOPQRS
abcdefghijklmnopqrstuvw

PICAS
| 6 | 12 | 18 | 24 | 30 | 36 |

PALATINO

Desktop Publishing: Design Basics

48 point

ABCDEFGHIJKLMNO
abcdefghijklmnop

60 point

ABCDEFGHIJKL
abcdefghijklm

72 point

ABCDEFGHIJ
abcdefghijk

PICAS
| | 6 | 12 | 18 | 24 | 30 | 36 |

PALATINO

14 point

ABCDEFGHIJKLMNOPQRSTUVWXYZ
abcdefghijklmnopqrstuvwxyz

18 point

ABCDEFGHIJKLMNOPQRSTUVWXYZ
abcdefghijklmnopqrstuvwxyz

24 point

ABCDEFGHIJKLMNOPQRSTUVWXYZ
abcdefghijklmnopqrstuvwxyz

30 point

ABCDEFGHIJKLMNOPQRSTUVWXYZ
abcdefghijklmnopqrstuvwxyz

36 point

ABCDEFGHIJKLMNOPQRS
abcdefghijklmnopqrstuvw

PICAS   6   12   18   24   30   36

PALATINO BOLD

Desktop Publishing: Design Basics

48 point

ABCDEFGHIJKLMNO
abcdefghijklmnop

60 point

ABCDEFGHIJKL
abcdefghijklm

72 point

ABCDEFGHIJ
abcdefghijk

PICAS | 6 | 12 | 18 | 24 | 30 | 36

PALATINO BOLD

14 point

ABCDEFGHIJKLMNOPQRSTUVWXYZ
abcdefghijklmnopqrstuvwxyz

18 point

ABCDEFGHIJKLMNOPQRSTUVWXYZ
abcdefghijklmnopqrstuvwxyz

24 point

ABCDEFGHIJKLMNOPQRSTUVWXYZ
abcdefghijklmnopqrstuvwxyz

30 point

ABCDEFGHIJKLMNOPQRSTUVWXYZ
abcdefghijklmnopqrstuvwxyz

36 point

ABCDEFGHIJKLMNOPQRS
abcdefghijklmnopqrstuvw

PICAS

| 6 | 12 | 18 | 24 | 30 | 36 |

PALATINO ITALIC

48 point

ABCDEFGHIJKLMNO
abcdefghijklmnop

60 point

ABCDEFGHIJKL
abcdefghijklm

72 point

ABCDEFGHIJ
abcdefghijk

PICAS

| 6 | 12 | 18 | 24 | 30 | 36 |

PALATINO ITALIC

14 point

ABCDEFGHIJKLMNOPQRSTUVWXYZ
abcdefghijklmnopqrstuvwxyz

18 point

ABCDEFGHIJKLMNOPQRSTUVWXYZ
abcdefghijklmnopqrstuvwxyz

24 point

ABCDEFGHIJKLMNOPQRSTUVWXYZ
abcdefghijklmnopqrstuvwxyz

30 point

ABCDEFGHIJKLMNOPQRSTUVWXYZ
abcdefghijklmnopqrstuvwxyz

36 point

ABCDEFGHIJKLMNOPQRS
abcdefghijklmnopqrstuvw

PICAS

| 6 | 12 | 18 | 24 | 30 | 36 |

PALATINO BOLD ITALIC

Desktop Publishing: Design Basics

48 point

ABCDEFGHIJKLMNO
abcdefghijklmnop

60 point

ABCDEFGHIJKL
abcdefghijklm

72 point

ABCDEFGHIJ
abcdefghijk

PICAS

| 6 | 12 | 18 | 24 | 30 | 36 |

PALATINO BOLD ITALIC

14 point

ABCDEFGHIJKLMNOPQRSTUVWXYZ
abcdefghijklmnopqrstuvwxyz

18 point

ABCDEFGHIJKLMNOPQRSTUVWXYZ
abcdefghijklmnopqrstuvwxyz

24 point

ABCDEFGHIJKLMNOPQRSTUVWXYZ
abcdefghijklmnopqrstuvwxyz

30 point

ABCDEFGHIJKLMNOPQRSTUVWXYZ
abcdefghijklmnopqrstuvwxyz

36 point

ABCDEFGHIJKLMNOPQRS
abcdefghijklmnopqrstuvw

PICAS
| 6 | 12 | 18 | 24 | 30 | 36 |

TIMES

Desktop Publishing: Design Basics

48 point

ABCDEFGHIJKLMNO
abcdefghijklmnop

60 point

ABCDEFGHIJKL
abcdefghijklm

72 point

ABCDEFGHIJ
abcdefghijk

PICAS

| 6 | 12 | 18 | 24 | 30 | 36 |

TIMES

14 point

ABCDEFGHIJKLMNOPQRSTUVWXYZ
abcdefghijklmnopqrstuvwxyz

18 point

ABCDEFGHIJKLMNOPQRSTUVWXYZ
abcdefghijklmnopqrstuvwxyz

24 point

ABCDEFGHIJKLMNOPQRSTUVWXYZ
abcdefghijklmnopqrstuvwxyz

30 point

ABCDEFGHIJKLMNOPQRSTUVWXYZ
abcdefghijklmnopqrstuvwxyz

36 point

ABCDEFGHIJKLMNOPQRS
abcdefghijklmnopqrstuvw

PICAS

| 6 | 12 | 18 | 24 | 30 | 36 |

TIMES BOLD

Desktop Publishing: Design Basics

48 point

ABCDEFGHIJKLMNO
abcdefghijklmnop

60 point

ABCDEFGHIJKL
abcdefghijklm

72 point

ABCDEFGHIJ
abcdefghijk

PICAS | 6 | 12 | 18 | 24 | 30 | 36

TIMES BOLD

14 point

ABCDEFGHIJKLMNOPQRSTUVWXYZ
abcdefghijklmnopqrstuvwxyz

18 point

ABCDEFGHIJKLMNOPQRSTUVWXYZ
abcdefghijklmnopqrstuvwxyz

24 point

ABCDEFGHIJKLMNOPQRSTUVWXYZ
abcdefghijklmnopqrstuvwxyz

30 point

ABCDEFGHIJKLMNOPQRSTUVWXYZ
abcdefghijklmnopqrstuvwxyz

36 point

ABCDEFGHIJKLMNOPQRS
abcdefghijklmnopqrstuvw

PICAS | 6 | 12 | 18 | 24 | 30 | 36

TIMES ITALIC

48 point

ABCDEFGHIJKLMNO
abcdefghijklmnop

60 point

ABCDEFGHIJKL
abcdefghijklm

72 point

ABCDEFGHIJ
abcdefghijk

PICAS

| 6 | 12 | 18 | 24 | 30 | 36 |

TIMES ITALIC

14 point

ABCDEFGHIJKLMNOPQRSTUVWXYZ
abcdefghijklmnopqrstuvwxyz

18 point

ABCDEFGHIJKLMNOPQRSTUVWXYZ
abcdefghijklmnopqrstuvwxyz

24 point

ABCDEFGHIJKLMNOPQRSTUVWXYZ
abcdefghijklmnopqrstuvwxyz

30 point

ABCDEFGHIJKLMNOPQRSTUVWXYZ
abcdefghijklmnopqrstuvwxyz

36 point

ABCDEFGHIJKLMNOPQRS
abcdefghijklmnopqrstuvw

PICAS | 6 | 12 | 18 | 24 | 30 | 36

TIMES BOLD ITALIC

Desktop Publishing: Design Basics

48 point

ABCDEFGHIJKLMNO
abcdefghijklmnop

60 point

ABCDEFGHIJKL
abcdefghijklm

72 point

ABCDEFGHIJ
abcdefghijk

PICAS | 6 | 12 | 18 | 24 | 30 | 36

TIMES BOLD ITALIC

14 point

ABCDEFGHIJKLMNOPQRSTUVWXYZ
abcdefghijklmnopqrstuvwxyz

18 point

ABCDEFGHIJKLMNOPQRSTUVWXYZ
abcdefghijklmnopqrstuvwxyz

24 point

ABCDEFGHIJKLMNOPQRSTUVWXYZ
abcdefghijklmnopqrstuvwxyz

30 point

ABCDEFGHIJKLMNOPQRSTUVWXYZ
abcdefghijklmnopqrstuvwxyz

36 point

ABCDEFGHIJKLMNOPQRS
abcdefghijklmnopqrstuvw

PICAS

| 6 | 12 | 18 | 24 | 30 | 36 |

ZAPF CHANCERY

Desktop Publishing: Design Basics 119

48 point

ABCDEFGHIJKLMNO
abcdefghijklmnop

60 point

ABCDEFGHIJKL
abcdefghijklm

72 point

ABCDEFGHIJ
abcdefghijk

PICAS

| 6 | 12 | 18 | 24 | 30 | 36 |

ZAPF CHANCERY

ZAPF DINGBATS